MERCURY READER

a custom publication

Peter Bruni
English 100

College of San Mateo

Pearson Learning Solutions

New York   Boston   San Francisco
London   Toronto   Sydney   Tokyo   Singapore   Madrid
Mexico City   Munich   Paris   Cape Town   Hong Kong   Montreal

Senior Vice President, Editorial and Marketing: Patrick F. Boles
Senior Sponsoring Editor: Natalie Danner
Development Editor: Mary Kate Paris
Assistant Editor: Jill Johnson
Operations Manager: Eric M. Kenney
Production Manager: Jennifer Berry
Rights Manager: Jillian Santos
Art Director: Renée Sartell
Cover Designers: Kristen Kiley, Blythe Russo, Tess Mattern, and Renée Sartell

Cover Art: "Gigantia Mountains & Sea of Cortes," by R.G.K. Photography, Copyright © Tony Stone Images; "Dime," courtesy of the Shaw Collection; "Open Book On Table Edge w/Pencil," courtesy of PhotoAlto Photography/Veer Incorporated; "Open Book On Table Near Table's Corner," courtesy of Fancy Photography/Veer Incorporated; "Scrabble Pieces and a Die," by G. Herbst, courtesy of PlainPicture Photography/Veer Incorporated; "Binary codes in bowls," by John Still, courtesy of Photographer's Choice/Getty Images; "Close-up of an open book," courtesy of Glowimages/Getty Images; "College Students Sitting At Tables," courtesy of Blend/PunchStock; "Red and blue circles," courtesy of Corbis Images; "Laptop screen showing photograph of landscape," courtesy of Martin Holtcamp/Getty Images; "Apples flying," courtesy of Arne Morgenstern/Getty Images.

Printed in the United States of America.

Please visit our website at *www.pearsoncustom.com.*

Attention bookstores: For permission to return any unsold stock, contact us at *pe-uscustomreturns@pearson.com.*

Pearson Learning Solutions, 501 Boylston Street, Suite 900, Boston, MA 02116
A Pearson Education Company
www.pearsoned.com

ISBN 10: 0-558-88805-4
ISBN 13: 978-0-558-88805-3

General Editors

Janice Neuleib
Illinois State University

Kathleen Shine Cain
Merrimack College

Stephen Ruffus
Salt Lake Community College

Contents

A Word About Honesty

The following is adapted from the Modern Language Association's *MLA Handbook for Writers of Research Papers*. New York: MLA, 1995: 26–29.

Intellectual Dishonesty

Intellectual dishonesty is demonstrated in the following ways:

Theft of a phrase or sentence
- repeating another's sentences without quotation and citation
- adopting and passing off a particularly apt phrase without quotation and citation

Theft of an argument or idea
- paraphrasing someone else's argument without attribution or citation
- presenting someone else's line of thinking in the development of a thesis without attribution or citation

You are being intellectually dishonest when you give the impression that you have written or thought something that you have in fact borrowed from another. Although a writer may use another person's words and thoughts, these phrases and ideas must be acknowledged as coming from another's work.

Note the difference in the four points listed above. When you use exact words from another, you must use quotation marks and cite the source. When you paraphrase or present another writer's arguments, you must either attribute your ideas to the source (As Will Shakespeare said etc.), or you must cite the source.

Note:

Sometimes students argue that they did not know that they could not use another's ideas without attribution or citation. Now you know.

Cheating

Students who copy from the work of other students or ask other students to do their work for them are, of course, guilty of cheating. Cheating will endanger your whole career. Do not do it.

Note:

If you are workshopping your work with your teacher and your class, you will not be tempted to cheat, since everyone will see your essays develop, and you will see everyone else's essays develop. Two of the most important parts of a writing class are learning to give intelligent feedback to others about their writing and using their feedback to improve your writing. This kind of interaction guarantees that you are doing your own work both in producing text and responding to others' texts.

The distinction between theft and cheating is more elaborately explained in an essay by Rebecca Moore Howard ["Sexuality, Textuality: The Cultural Work of Plagiarism," *College English*, 62 (March 2000): 473–491] and in Jo Anne Pagano's book *Exiles and Communities: Teaching in the Patriarchal Wilderness*, New York: SUNY, 1990.

How to Mark a Book

Mortimer Adler

Mortimer Adler (1902–2001) received his Ph.D. from Columbia University in 1928. A conservative thinker, Adler advocated education based on the "truths" found in the classical works of Western civilization. Many academic intellectuals have scorned his simple formulas for progress, but the larger culture has often embraced his ideas, as his post as chairman of the editorial board of the Encyclopedia Britannica *indicated. His Great Books project, for which he is widely known, resulted in the publication and wide circulation of handsome bound sets of important works of world literature. As you read his essay on how to mark a book, you will see a man who thought that the world is, or ought to be, clear and simple.*

1 You know you have to read "between the lines" to get the most out of anything. I want to persuade you to do something equally important in the course of your reading. I want to persuade you to "write between the lines." Unless you do, you are not likely to do the most efficient kind of reading.

I contend, quite bluntly, that marking up a book is not an act of mutilation but of love.

You shouldn't mark up a book which isn't yours. Librarians (or your friends) who lend you books expect you to keep them clean, and you should. If you decide that I am right about the usefulness of marking books, you will have to buy them. Most of the world's great books are available today, in reprint editions, at less than a dollar.

There are two ways in which you can own a book. The first is the property right you establish by paying for it, just as you pay for clothes and furniture. But this act of purchase is only the prelude to possession. Full ownership comes only when you have made it a part of yourself, and the best way to make yourself a part of it is by writing in it. An illustration may make the point clear. You buy a beefsteak and transfer it from the butcher's ice-box to your own. But you do not own the beefsteak in the most important sense until you consume it and get it into your bloodstream. I am arguing that books, too, must be absorbed in your bloodstream to do you any good.

5   Confusion about what it means to *own* a book leads people to a   5
false reverence for paper, binding, and type—a respect for the physical thing—the craft of the printer rather than the genius of the author. They forget that it is possible for a man to acquire the idea, to possess the beauty, which a great book contains, without staking his claim by pasting his bookplate inside the cover. Having a fine library doesn't prove that its owner has a mind enriched by books; it proves nothing more than that he, his father, or his wife, was rich enough to buy them.

There are three kinds of book owners. The first has all the standard sets and best-sellers—unread, untouched. (This deluded individual owns woodpulp and ink, not books.) The second has a great many books—a few of them read through, most of them dipped into, but all of them as clean and shiny as the day they were bought. (This person would probably like to make books his own, but is restrained by a false respect for their physical appearance.) The third has a few books or many—everyone of them dog-eared and dilapidated, shaken and loosened by continual use, marked and scribbled in from front to back. (This man owns books.)

Is it false respect, you may ask, to preserve intact and unblemished a beautifully printed book, an elegantly bound edition? Of course not. I'd no more scribble all over a first edition of *Paradise Lost* than I'd give my baby a set of crayons and an original Rembrandt! I wouldn't mark up a painting or a statue. Its soul, so to speak, is inseparable from its body. And the beauty of a rare edition or of a richly manufactured volume is like that of a painting or a statue.

But the soul of a book *can* be separated from its body. A book is more like the score of a piece of music than it is like a painting. No great musician confuses a symphony with the printed sheets of music. Arturo Toscanini reveres Brahms, but Toscanini's score of the C-minor Symphony is so thoroughly marked up that no one but the maestro himself can read it. The reason why a great conductor makes notations on his musical scores—marks them up again and again each time he returns to study them—is the reason why you should mark your books.

If your respect for magnificent binding or typography gets in the way, buy yourself a cheap edition and pay your respects to the author.

Why is marking up a book indispensable to reading? First, it keeps you awake. (And I don't mean merely conscious; I mean wide awake.) In the second place, reading, if it is active, is thinking, and thinking tends to express itself in words, spoken or written. The marked book is usually the thought-through book. Finally, writing helps you re-member the thoughts you had, or the thoughts the author expressed. Let me develop these three points.

If reading is to accomplish anything more than passing time, it must be active. You can't let your eyes glide across the lines of a book and come up with an understanding of what you have read. Now an ordinary piece of light fiction, like say, *Gone With the Wind,* doesn't require the most active kind of reading. The books you read for plea-sure can be read in a state of relaxation, and nothing is lost. But a great book, rich in ideas and beauty, a book that raises and tries to answer great fundamental questions, demands the most active reading of which you are capable. You don't absorb the ideas of John Dewey the way you absorb the crooning of Mr. Vallee. You have to reach for them. That you cannot do while you're asleep.

If, when you've finished reading a book, the pages are filled with your notes, you know that you read actively. The most famous *active* reader of great books I know is President Hutchins, of the University of Chicago. He also has the hardest schedule of business activities of any man I know. He invariably reads with a pencil, and sometimes, when he picks up a book and pencil in the evening, he finds himself, instead of making intelligent notes, drawing what he calls "caviar fac-tories" on the margins. When that happens, he puts the book down. He knows he's too tired to read, and he's just wasting time.

But, you may ask, why is writing necessary? Well, the physical act of writing, with your own hand, brings words and sentences more sharply before your mind and preserves them better in your memory. To set down your reaction to important words and sentences you have read, and the questions they have raised in your mind, is to preserve those reactions and sharpen those questions.

Even if you wrote on a scratch pad, and threw the paper away when you had finished writing, your grasp of the book would be surer. But you don't have to throw the paper away. The margins (top and bottom, as well as side), the end-papers, the very space between the lines, are all available. They aren't sacred. And, best of all, your marks and notes become an integral part of the book and stay there forever. You can pick up the book the following week or year, and there are all your points of agreement, disagreement, doubt, and inquiry. It's like resuming an interrupted conversation with the advantage of being able to pick up where you left off.

And that is exactly what reading a book should be: a conversation between you and the author. Presumably he knows more about the subject than you do; naturally, you'll have the proper humility as you approach him. But don't let anybody tell you that a reader is supposed to be solely on the receiving end. Understanding is a two-way operation; learning doesn't consist in being an empty receptacle. The learner has to question himself and question the teacher. He even has to argue with the teacher, once he understands what the teacher is saying. And marking a book is literally an expression of your differences, or agreements of opinion, with the author.

15   There are all kinds of devices for marking a book intelligently and 15
fruitfully. Here's the way I do it:

1. *Underlining:* Of major points, of important or forceful statements.
2. *Vertical lines at the margin:* To emphasize a statement already underlined.
3. *Star, asterisk, or other doo-dad at the margin:* To be used sparingly, to emphasize the ten or twenty most important statements in the book. (You may want to fold the bottom corner of each page on which you use such marks. It won't hurt the sturdy paper on which most modern books are printed, and you will be able to take the book off the shelf at any time and, by opening it at the folded corner page, refresh your recollection of the book.)
4. *Numbers in the margin:* To indicate the sequence of points the author makes in developing a single argument.
20 5. *Numbers of other pages in the margin:* To indicate where else in the 20
book the author made points relevant to the point marked; to tie up the ideas in a book, which, though they may be separated by many pages, belong together.
6. *Circling of key words or phrases.*
7. *Writing in the margin, or at the top or bottom of the page, for the sake of:* Recording questions (and perhaps answers) which a passage raised in your mind; reducing a complicated discussion to a simple statement; recording the sequence of major points right through the books. I use the end-papers at the back of the book

to make a personal index of the author's points in the order of their appearance.

The front end-papers are, to me, the most important. Some people reserve them for a fancy bookplate. I reserve them for fancy thinking. After I have finished reading the book and making my personal index on the back end-papers, I turn to the front and try to outline the book, not page by page, or point by point (I've already done that at the back), but as an integrated structure, with a basic unity and an order of parts. This outline is, to me, the measure of my understanding of the work.

If you're a die-hard anti-book-marker, you may object that the margins, the space between the lines, and the end-papers don't give you room enough. All right. How about using a scratch pad slightly smaller than the page-size of the book—so that the edges of the sheets won't protrude? Make your index, outlines, and even your notes on the pad, and then insert these sheets permanently inside the front and back covers of the book.

25 Or, you may say that this business of marking books is going to 25 slow up your reading. It probably will. That's one of the reasons for doing it. Most of us have been taken in by the notion that speed of reading is a measure of our intelligence. There is no such thing as the right speed for intelligent reading. Some things should be read quickly and effortlessly, and some should be read slowly and even laboriously. The sign of intelligence in reading is the ability to read different things differently according to their worth. In the case of good books, the point is not to see how many of them you can get through, but rather how many can get through you—how many you can make your own. A few friends are better than a thousand acquaintances. If this be your aim, as it should be, you will not be impatient if it takes more time and effort to read a great book than it does a newspaper.

You may have one final objection to marking books. You can't lend them to your friends because nobody else can read them without being distracted by your notes. Furthermore, you won't want to lend them because a marked copy is a kind of intellectual diary, and lending it is almost like giving your mind away.

If your friend wishes to read your *Plutarch's Lives,* "Shakespeare," or *The Federalist Papers,* tell him gently but firmly to buy a copy. You will lend him your car or your coat—but your books are as much a part of you as your head or your heart.

Questions on Meaning

1. Paraphrase the point Adler is making in comparing buying a book to buying a beefsteak.
2. Critique Adler's comparison of a book's meaning to the concept of a soul. Look up the word *soul* in a dictionary and organize your critique by the points of the dictionary definitions.
3. Explain Adler's assertion that "There is no such thing as the right speed for intelligent reading."

Questions on Rhetorical Strategy and Style

1. Where is Adler's description of how to mark a book least clear? Explain why.
2. Adler's style is based on very short sentences. Try combining the sentences in a single paragraph (e.g., the one beginning, "There are two ways in which you can own a book . . ."). Compare your revision with the original and describe the alteration in tone you note from the longer sentences.

Writing Assignments

1. Write an essay that describes a few of the most influential books you've ever read. Did you read them actively, as Adler recommends? How did they affect your thinking or behavior?
2. Compile a list of five books you think you should read but haven't yet. Write an essay that tells the story of how you found out about these books.

Documentation in the Humanities: MLA Style

Documentation is like traffic signs and signals: Everyone in a culture agrees to use them in a certain way so that nobody gets hurt. Communities of readers and writers do the same thing: They agree to identify their sources according to a given set of rules. There are several forms of documentation for particular areas of study and specific journals.

The Modern Language Association of America is an international organization of teachers and researchers dedicated to the study and teaching of language and literature. Many humanities departments in schools and colleges as well as a host of journals and magazines require that writers use the MLA style when presenting a manuscript. The details of MLA style are presented in two books, the *MLA Handbook for Writers of Research Papers*, used mostly by high school and undergraduate college students; and the *MLA Style Manual and Guide to Scholarly Publishing*, used by graduate students, scholars, and professional writers).

MLA Manuscript Format

In addition to the many, many specifics of preparing a manuscript in MLA style, the following general rules apply.

Page layout:

- Use standard 8-1/2 by 11 paper and standard typeface. Avoid odd typefaces or other unusual variations available with word processing.
- Place name, date, and course information in the upper left-hand corner of the first page; double-space before the centered title.
- Double-space between lines.
- Leave at least one inch margins.

- Place page numbers in the upper right-hand corner, one half inch from the top of the paper; include your last name before the number for identification.

In the body of the paper:

- Cite sources in the text, not in footnotes or endnotes.
- Don't use punctuation between the author's name and the page number in a citation.
- Cite the page number(s) of direct quotations in in-text citations.
- Indent the first line of each paragraph five spaces.
- Indent quotations more than four typed lines ten spaces; omit the quotation marks.
- Leave one space after all punctuation; MLA allows either a single or a double space after periods or question and exclamation marks.
- Form a dash with two hyphens, using no spaces.

In the list of sources:

- Center the words "Works Cited" on the top of the page.
- List sources alphabetically by author's last name. If there is no author, alphabetize by book or selection title.
- Use hanging indentation (first line flush left against the margin, second and subsequent lines indented).
- Separate items in a citation (author, title, place and date of publication) with periods.
- If the city of publication is not easily recognizable, add a two-letter abbreviation for the state.

IN-TEXT CITATION

1. Author named in text
If the author is named in the text, only page numbers are given.

```
Stephen Jay Gould discusses the power of
scientific drawings (18).
```

2. Author not named in text
When the author is not named in the text, the name appears in the notation.

```
Deep time appears as a new concept in
Lavoisier (Gould 22).
```

3. Two or three authors
Use only the last names of the authors.

```
Scharton and Neuleib claim that professors
change when they work with writing centers
(65).
```

4. Four or more authors
All four authors may be named, or author number one and "et al." (Latin for "et alia" which means "and others") may be referenced in the text or in parentheses.

```
Duin, Lammers, Mason, and Graves suggest that
mentors with much teaching experience will
give more help than mentors who have taught
little (143).
```

```
Mentors with much teaching experience will
give more help than mentors who have taught
little (Duin et al. 143).
```

5. Unknown author
The title substitutes for the author's name in the text or in parentheses.

```
"The Twin Corbies" refers to crows (119).
```

6. Corporate author

A corporate author can be named in either the text or in the parentheses.

```
Illinois State University notes that it
employs 264 professors (1).
```

7. Two or more works by the same author

When two or more works by one author appear on the Works Cited page, either name the work in the text, or include a short form of the title in the parentheses.

```
In "The Gift of Insight," Neuleib and
Scharton explain the complexities of type
preference (197).
```

If author and shortened form both appear in parentheses, use this form:

```
(Neuleib and Scharton, "Insight" 197).
```

8. A source quoted in another source

To show that one author is quoting another, use the abbreviation "qtd. in."

```
Flower notes that "research in composition
shows an alternative picture of how knowledge
can be developed" (qtd. in Neuleib and
Scharton 54).
```

9. Novel, play, or poem

Give the title if not mentioned in text when the work is first referred to, then follow with specific information as listed below.

Novel: part or chapter
```
Ged said, "I fear what follows behind me"
(A Wizard of Earthsea 117: ch. 6).
```

Play: act and scene and line numbers in Arabic numerals
```
"He waxes desperate with imagination," cries
Horatio (Hamlet 1.4.87).
```

Poem: refer to the part (if applicable) and line numbers
```
"Surely some revelation is at hand," muses
Yeats's "The Second Coming" (10).
```

10. Work in an anthology
Cite the author's name, not the editor's name.

```
In his essay "On Stories," Lewis observes
that "No book is really worth reading at the
age of ten which is not equally worth reading
at the age of fifty" (100).
```

11. Entire work
Name the author in the text or note in parentheses.

```
Freire was introduced to North American
scholars in Freire for the Classroom (Shor).
```

WORKS CITED

Books

1. One author
```
LeGuin, Ursula K. A Wizard of Earthsea. New
    York: Ace, 1968.
```

2. Two or three authors
```
Scharton, Maurice, and Janice Neuleib. Inside/
    Out: A Guide to Writing. Needham Heights,
    MA: Allyn & Bacon, 1992.
```

3. More than three authors or editors
```
Lawson, Bruce, et al., eds. Encountering Stu-
    dent Texts. Urbana: NCTE, 1989.
```

4. Editor
```
Hooper, Walter, ed. The Letters of C. S. Lewis.
    New York: Macmillan, 1979.
```

5. Author with editor

> Tolkien, J.R.R. <u>The Tolkien Reader</u>. Ed.
> Christopher Tolkien. New York: Ballantine,
> 1966.

6. Unknown author

> <u>Primary Colors</u>. New York: Random House, 1996.

7. Corporate author

> Illinois State University. <u>Facts 1998-9</u>. Nor-
> mal, IL: Illinois State UP, 1999.

8. Two or more works by the same author

> Lewis, C. S. <u>The Lion, the Witch, and the
> Wardrobe</u>. New York: Macmillan, 1950.
>
> ---. <u>The Magician's Nephew</u>. New York: Macmil-
> lan, 1955.

9. Translation

> Tolstoy, L. N. <u>Anna Karenina</u>. Trans. Rosemary
> Edmunds. New York: Viking, 1954.

10. Work in an anthology

> Walsh, Chad. "The Reeducation of the Fearful
> Pilgrim." <u>The Longing for a Form</u>. Ed.
> Peter J. Schakel. Kent, OH: Kent State UP,
> 1977. 64-72.

Periodicals

11. Newspaper article
    (signed)

> Flick, Bill. "This Year in History." <u>Daily
> Pantagraph</u> 31 Dec. 1998: A14.

(unsigned)
"Honda Motor Recalls Several Models to Fix
    Ball-Joint Assembly." <u>Wall Street Journal</u>
    13 May 1999: B14.

12. Magazine article
(signed)
Gould, Stephen Jay. "Capturing the Center."
    <u>Natural History</u> Dec. 1998: 14+.

(unsigned)
"College Can Give You Grief." <u>Psychology
    Today</u> Oct. 1998: 20.

13. Journal article
(with continuous page numbering from issue to issue within a
year)
Fleckenstein, Kristie. "Writing Bodies." <u>Col-
    lege English</u> 61 (1999): 281-306.

(with each issue paged separately)
Becker, Becky K. "Women Who Choose: The Theme
    of Mothering in Selected Dramas." <u>American
    Drama</u> 6.2 (1997): 43+.

[note that "6.2" means vol. 6, issue #2]

Other Sources

14. The Bible
<u>The New International Bible</u>. Colorado
    Springs: International Bible Society,
    1972.

[The King James Bible need not be named or underlined. You
need only note chapter and verse in parentheses in the text
(Matt:12.1-3). Translations of the Bible other than King James
should be identified and underlined.]

15. Letter to the editor

    White, Curt. Letter. <u>The Vidette</u>. 18 Feb.
      1999: 6.

16. Personal or telephone interview

    Kay, Martha. Personal interview. 10 Mar.
      1999.

17. Record, tape, or CD

    Kingston Trio. <u>Greatest Hits</u>. Curb Records,
      1991.

Electronic Sources

These sources include a variety of types of communication: personal e-mail between persons or among private group members, listservs among several individuals with common work or interests, or news groups that serve associations or subscribers. The World Wide Web connects the individual to a wider community, including businesses and other commercial groups. For all these sources, documentation should be used consistently. Note that the second date is always the date a website was accessed while the first date is the time of publication.

18. Professional site

    <u>NCTE Home Page</u>. 6 January 2004. National Coun-
      cil of Teachers of English. 4 Mar. 2004
      <http://www.ncte.org>.

19. A personal site

    Neuleib, Janice Witherspoon. Home page. Illi-
      nois State University. 26 Feb. 2004 <http://
      www.ilstu.edu/~jneuleib>.

20. A book

    Crane, Stephen. <u>The Red Badge of Courage</u>. Gut-
      tenberg Project. <u>University of California
      Berkeley Archives</u>. 4 Sept. 1996. Sunsite

Berkeley. 4 Mar. 2004 <http://sunsite.
berkeley.edu/Literature/Crane/RedBadge/>.

21. A poem
Dickinson, Emily. "A Narrow Fellow in the
Grass," <u>Poetry Archive</u>.
<http://www.emule.com/poetry<.

22. An article in a reference database
"On 'Behave.'" <u>Oxford English Dictionary On-
line</u>. Second Edition. 1989. Oxford English
Dictionary. 5 Mar. 2004
<http://dictionary.oed.com/cgi/entry/00019662>.

23. An article in a journal
Applebee, Arthur N., and Judith A. Langer.
"Discussion-Based Approaches to Student Understanding: Classroom Instruction in the
Middle School Classroom." <u>American Education Research Journal</u> 40:3 (2003). 2 Mar.
2004. <http://www.ncte.org/about/research/
articles/115102.htm>.

24. An article in a magazine
Perkins, Sid. "Avalanche." <u>Science News On Line</u>
2 Mar. 2002. 16 Feb. 2004 <http://www. sci-
encenews.org/articles/20020302/bob14.asp>.

25. A review
Traister, Rebecca. "Is 'The Sopranos' a Chick
Flick?" Rev. of <u>The Sopranos TV Series</u>.<u>Salon</u>
6 Mar. 2004. 8 Mar. 2004. <www.salon.com
.mwt/feature/2004/03/06/carmela_soprano/
index_mp.html>

26. A posting to a discussion group

Hesse, Doug. "What Makes a College Good." Online
posting. 5 Nov. 2003. ISU Teach. 7 Mar. 2004
<isuteach@listserv.ilstu.edu>.

27. A personal e-mail message

Neuleib, Janice. "Collaborative MR Chapter."
E-mail to Katherine Gretz. 19 Feb. 2004.

Narration

Throughout most of our lives, we read, write, listen to, and tell stories. Our religious and cultural values are often passed on through stories, as is our history. And of course, stories have always entertained us.

Narration is the act of relating a story; the story itself is called a *narrative*. While narrative is a complex form with a variety of purposes, most meaningful narratives, particularly essays, have a point. Fairy tales, religious stories, and historical narratives are all told in order to drive home a point—about behavior, belief, or national identity. To convey that point, the writer of narrative must pay attention to the *conventions* of narration.

Often, the point of a narrative essay is stated or implied in the first paragraph, but sometimes the writer waits until the end. The clarity of that point is dependent on the writer's ability to *show* the reader what happens rather than simply *tell* about the action. A writer can achieve this goal by paying careful attention to organization, detail, and word choice. Organization in a narrative is almost always chronological; the story is told in a specific time sequence. Such organization allows readers to follow the action without becoming confused. Organization is supported by clear, precise details; readers must be able to envision the action in order to understand the story. These details are created by descriptive word choice, or diction. The following narrative, from Maya Angelou's "Graduation," illustrates these features:

> *Amazingly the great day finally dawned and I was out of bed before I knew it. I threw open the back door to see it more clearly, but Momma said, "Sister, come away from that door and put your robe on." I hoped the memory of that morning would never leave me. Sunlight was itself young, and the day had none of the insistence maturity would bring it in a few hours. In my robe and barefoot in the backyard, under cover of going to see about my new beans, I gave myself up to the*

gentle warmth and thanked God that no matter what evil I had done in my life He had allowed me to live to see this day. Somewhere in my fatalism I had expected to die, accidentally, and never have the chance to walk up the stairs in the auditorium and gracefully receive my hard-earned diploma. Out of God's merciful bosom I had won reprieve. Bailey came out in his robe and gave me a box wrapped in Christmas paper. He said he had saved his money for months to pay for it. It felt like a box of chocolates, but I knew Bailey wouldn't save money to buy candy when we had all we could want under our noses. He was as proud of the gift as I. It was a soft-leather-bound copy of a collection of poems by Edgar Allan Poe, or, as Bailey and I called him, "Eap." I turned to "Annabel Lee" and we walked up and down the garden rows, the cool dirt between our toes, reciting the beautifully sad lines.

Notice how Angelou organizes her story in simple chronological order: she goes to the door in the early morning, relishes the sweetness of the day, is joined by her brother, receives his gift, and then recites poetry with him as they walk through the garden. The author also brings readers into the narrative through the use of specific details: the warmth of the day is "gentle," Bailey's present is wrapped in Christmas paper and feels like a box of chocolates, the book is bound in soft leather, and she and her brother feel "the cool dirt between [their] toes." Both organization and detail, supported by precise diction, make the scene real to readers.

While narration may be the primary rhetorical strategy employed in an essay, it may also be used in an essay employing a different strategy. For example, a persuasive essay might use a brief story to support its argument, or a cause-and-effect essay might use a narrative to illustrate a sequence of events. In these cases, narrative is used as an *example*. In fact, one could argue that the narrative "Graduation" is an extended example of the evils of segregation and the resilience of African Americans in the face of discrimination. As the excerpt illustrates, regardless of how it is used, an effective narrative will command the reader's attention.

Description

If you have ever tried to recreate for someone who has not seen it a sunset over the ocean, an unusual animal in a zoo, or a building with unique architectural features, then you know how important description is. When a writer describes something, she or he creates an image with words. In order to do that, the writer must also be a careful observer of the world around him or her. Sometimes writers offer readers *objective* descriptions, recreating for the reader, in precise detail, the image as it might appear to anyone observing it. But sometimes writers create *subjective* descriptions, reproducing the image as it appears to the writer, including the writer's emotional response to the image. A sunset, for example, might be described purely in terms of the colors of the sky, the size of the sun relative to the horizon, and the time required for the sun to sink below the horizon. Subjectively, on the other hand, the sunset might be described as infusing the sky with hopeful illumination, or instilling in the observer a sense of peace, or creating in the observer an awe of nature.

In "Graduation," Angelou describes class valedictorian Henry Reed in objective terms, as "a small, very black boy with hooded eyes, a long, broad nose and an oddly shaped head." She describes the days preceding graduation, however, in subjective terms: "The faded beige of former times had been replaced with strong and sure colors. . . . Clouds that lazed across the sky were objects of great concern to me. Their shiftier shapes might have held a message that in my new happiness and with a little bit of time I'd soon decipher."

Whatever the description, there must be a *purpose* for presenting it, an impression that the writer wants to leave with the reader. That purpose might be simply to create an image in the reader's mind, as Angelou does in her description of the days before her graduation. But description may also be used in conjunction with other rhetorical strategies, for example, to describe an effect. Angelou does this in "Graduation" when she describes her feelings as she listens to the white speaker denigrating her people: "The man's dead words fell like bricks around the auditorium and too many settled in my belly. . . . Every girl in my row had found something new to do with her handkerchief. Some folded the tiny squares into love knots, some into triangles, but most were wadding them, then pressing them flat on their yellow laps." The vivid detail of this description shows the reader how Angelou and her classmates felt rather than simply telling the reader about it. The good writer of description will try to arouse the reader's senses—of sight, smell, touch, taste, hearing, and movement. Unlike narrative, a description rarely involves a time sequence (unless the thing described involves time) and arrangement is spatial rather than chronological. But like narrative, a description must include clear details if it is to be successful. A good description, as the Angelou examples illustrate, will leave the reader with the sense that he or she has experienced the image along with the writer.

Comparison and Contrast

One of the easiest ways for us to understand a thing is to consider it alongside something else, emphasizing either similarities, differences, or both. We are always making comparisons: of products, in order to determine which is the best buy; of restaurants, in order to determine which is most appropriate for a given occasion; of candidates for office, in order to determine which will best serve our interests. What these three examples illustrate is that we use comparison and contrast not for its own sake but to support a point. Thus, if you use this strategy in your writing, you should always keep the *point* of your comparison in mind.

Usually, the two subjects under comparison will have something in common; that common feature will constitute the basis for comparison. When you were deciding on a college, for example, you may have considered a large public university, a small private college, or a community college. These kinds of schools are quite different, but they all share at least one common basis for comparison: they are all institutions of higher education. When making comparisons, it is important to maintain the *same basis* for each subject being compared. For example, if you scrutinize the liberal arts *curriculum* of the first two schools, but then focus on the *location* of the third school, you have undermined your comparison by changing the basis. By focusing on the same qualities of each subject, you maintain that basis.

In "Graduation," Maya Angelou uses comparison and contrast briefly when she refers to Mr. Donleavy's speech praising the accomplishments of both white and African American children in the school district. In response to his words, she thinks, "The white kids were going to have a chance to become Galileos and Madame Curies and Edisons and Gaugins, and our boys (the girls weren't even in on it) would try to be Jesse Owenses and Joe Louises." In this case, the basis for comparison is the field in which children might hope to succeed.

Later in the essay, Angelou contrasts her appreciation of "Lift Ev'ry Voice and Sing," known as "the Negro National Anthem," to her response to Patrick Henry's "Give me liberty or give me death" speech:

> *Each child I know had learned ["Lift Ev'ry Voice"] with his ABC's and along with "Jesus Loves Me This I Know." But I personally had never heard it before. Never heard the words, despite the thousand of times I had sung them. Never thought they had anything to do with me. On the other hand, the words of Patrick Henry had made such an impression on me that I had been able to stretch myself tall and trembling and say, "I know not what course others may take, but as for me, give me liberty or give me death."*

Angelou's basis for comparison in this example is the child's misunderstanding of the relevance of famous words.

The Angelou examples represent *comparison* and *contrast* used in support of other rhetorical strategies (e.g., *narrative* and *persuasion*). At times, however, an entire essay can be written using the comparison-and-contrast strategy. In such essays, appropriate organization is essential. Most writers recognize two primary methods of organization for comparison and contrast: point-by-point or subject-by-subject. Consider the educational institutions mentioned earlier, for example: if you were to write an essay on the topic, you might organize your comparison by looking at curriculum, cost, and location of the institutions. For each of these categories, you would consider each school in turn. This is a point-by-point organization. But you might also choose to consider the individual school, focusing on curriculum, cost, and location of each before moving on to a discussion of the next school. This organization is subject-by-subject. In outline form, the two organizations would look like this:

Point-by-Point	Subject-by-Subject
Curriculum	Large Public University
large public university	curriculum
small private college	cost
community college	location
Cost	Small Private College
large public university	curriculum
small private college	cost
community college	location
Location	Community College
large public university	curriculum
small private college	cost
community college	location

Occasionally, a writer will combine the two organizing strategies. Regardless of the strategy you choose, establishing a *pattern* for the comparison will make the essay clearer and easier for the reader to understand.

Whether a comparison is used in support of another rhetorical strategy or presented as the primary strategy in an essay, the same guidelines apply: the comparison must have a *point*, it must operate on a common *basis*, and (in the case of an essay) it must be *organized* appropriately.

Cause and Effect

Whenever you try to answer the question "why?" you are engaging in cause-and-effect analysis. Sometimes the analysis is simple: If a car won't start on a winter morning, chances are the battery is too weak to get a cold engine moving. But often the analysis is complex: In 1991, when war broke out in the Balkans after the fall of the Soviet Union, the causes ranged from economics, to religion, to nationalism, to ideology. Cause and effect can be used in support of another rhetorical strategy, for example, *persuasion*. Or it can be used as the primary rhetorical strategy in an essay. Whether the strategy is used as a primary or supporting strategy, or whether it focuses primarily on causes or effects, the features of the strategy remain the same.

One of those features is the identification of causes as either *immediate* or *remote*. In the case of the Balkans, for example, one of the immediate causes of the fighting was ethnic divisions among inhabitants of the area. These divisions became apparent shortly after the end of Soviet domination of the region, and thus were easily recognizable as a cause of the conflict. But the situation cannot be understood fully without considering remote causes, some of which go back to the redrawing of national boundaries following World War I. Since this cause is found in the history of a conflict that occurred over sixty years earlier, it is not so obvious as the more immediate causes. Nonetheless, remote causes are sometimes even more significant than immediate causes in explaining an effect.

Maya Angelou analyzes both immediate and remote causes in "Graduation." The immediate cause, for example, of the graduates' discomfort at the beginning of the graduation ceremony is a change in the order of the program:

> *We remained standing for a brief minute [after singing the national anthem] before the choir director and the principal signaled to us, rather desperately I thought, to take our seats. The command was so unusual that our carefully rehearsed and smooth-running machine was thrown off.*

The effect of this change in the program is profound: "Finding my seat at last, I was overcome with a presentiment of worse things to come. Something unrehearsed, unplanned, was going to happen, and we were going to be made to look bad." Later, valedictorian Henry Reed's leading the graduates in singing the Negro National Anthem constitutes the immediate cause for renewed pride: "We were on top again. As always, again. We survived. . . . I was no longer simply a member of the proud graduating class of 1940; I was a proud member of the wonderful, beautiful Negro race."

Throughout "Graduation," however, Angelou also implies remote causes for the emotions she feels throughout the ceremony. When she contemplates how "awful" it is "to be a Negro and have no control over my life," she is referring to the seventy-five years of segregation that followed the end of the Civil War. When she listens to Donleavy recount the great improvements to be made to the white schools, she is referring to the deep-seated inequality foisted on African Americans in the South. And later, when she sings the praises of "Black known and unknown poets" whose tales and songs have sustained her race, she is referring to the ongoing struggle of African Americans to achieve freedom and dignity. The imposition of segregation after the Civil War, the inequality built into the Southern social fabric, and the simmering rebellion within the African American community—all of these constitute remote causes for the young Angelou's reactions on her graduation night.

Another feature of cause-and-effect analysis is the distinction between *primary* and *contributory* causes. While the primary cause of the lengthy Balkan war can be found in the tensions within the region itself, a contributory cause might be the rest of the world's failure to intervene early in the conflict. Similarly, the primary cause of Angelou's dismay during the graduation ceremony is the denigrating speech delivered by Edward Donleavy. A contributory cause is the reaction of the leaders of the African American community: the principal's normally powerful voice nearly fades into silence when he introduces Donleavy, and when the speaker's driver takes the principal's seat on the dais, confusion ensues and no one objects. The identification of immediate and remote, primary and contributory, causes enriches the analysis of complex issues.

By now it should be clear that cause-and-effect analysis normally includes multiple causes; it often includes multiple effects as well. Consider once again the Balkan war example: It has been determined that the conflict was the result of many causes. One of those causes, however, was itself responsible for more than just the Balkan war. The armistice that ended World War I not only set the stage for later conflict in the Balkans, but also resulted in conditions in Germany that led to the rise of Nazism under Adolf Hitler. In fact, an effect of a given cause often becomes the cause of yet another effect. The terms imposed on Germany after World War I, for example, resulted in humiliation and economic turmoil in that country. In turn, the national humiliation and deplorable economic conditions resulted in public unrest, which in turn resulted in the rise of the National Socialist, or Nazi Party. The rise of Nazism contributed to the outbreak of World War II in Europe.

In "Graduation," Donleavy's speech causes the young Angelou to ponder the injustices heaped on her people, which apprehension, in turn, causes her not to hear her name when she is called to the stage to receive her diploma. The change in the program caused by Donleavy's appearance causes the graduates to lose their composure, which results in valedictorian Henry Reed's decision to change the program yet again and sing the Negro National Anthem, which causes the graduates to regain not only their composure but their pride. These multiple causes and multiple effects make cause-and-effect analysis more complicated than other rhetorical strategies such as *description* or *comparison and contrast.*

The key to handling this complex strategy effectively lies in recognizing legitimate causes and effects. For a cause to be credible, it must be both *necessary* and *sufficient* to produce an effect. To illustrate this requirement, consider the simple example of the car that fails to start. In determining the cause of the problem, a mechanic checks under the hood. If all other parts of the engine are working, then a weak or dead battery is both a necessary and sufficient cause of the car's failure to start. Checking the engine, the mechanic is looking for connections or relationships to determine the cause of the problem. A car's failure to start is a mechanical or an electrical problem; therefore, the causes probably lie in the mechanical or electrical operations of the car. In a more complex problem such as determining the causes of the Balkan war, a historian will also look for connections and relationships, in this case economic conditions, nationalism, religious conflicts, and the history of the region. The mechanic and the historian are experts in their respective fields, so they are likely to avoid a common fallacy found in cause-and-effect analysis. Called *post-hoc reasoning*, this fallacy proceeds from the assumption that simply because a phenomenon or an event precedes another, the first is the cause of the second. If, for example, the owner of the car had lent it to a friend the day before, there is no reason why she should blame her friend for the problem; the two events may be merely *coincidental*.

In "Graduation," the arrival of an unanticipated speaker would not in itself constitute a necessary and sufficient cause for the turmoil that follows. It is Edward Donleavy's position as a white politician, as well as his treatment of both the dignitaries on the dais and the audience in the hall, that make his appearance a necessary and sufficient cause. Earlier in the essay, Angelou describes her youthful conviction that God would punish her evil deeds by somehow not allowing her to participate in graduation. Had she attributed the turmoil caused by Donleavy's speech to her own evil deeds, she would have been falling into a *post-hoc* fallacy.

Another common problem found in cause-and-effect analysis involves *oversimplification*. This problem usually results from a failure to appreciate the complexity of causes and effects. For example, an uninformed writer might attribute the rise of Nazism solely to the economic conditions in Germany during the 1930s, ignoring the simmering anti-Semitism in the country, the disputes over territory along the borders with Austria and France, the inefficiency of the government, and a number of other causes. When analyzing the causes of a particular event or phenomenon, it is necessary to consider a variety of causes—immediate *and* remote, primary *and* contributing.

An essay employing cause-and-effect analysis can be organized by first describing the effect and then analyzing the causes that led to it, or by analyzing the causes first and then concluding with the effect. The writer should make this choice based on what he or she wants to emphasize in the analysis. For example, a writer who wants to emphasize the *history* of the Balkan war might elaborate on the various causes before discussing the war itself, while a writer who wants to emphasize possible *solutions* to the conflict might begin by focusing on the conflict, and then analyzing the causes that led to it. As in essays employing other strategies, the approach taken by the writer should reflect both the topic and the purpose of the essay.

Classification and Division

When we walk into a supermarket, we see individual items classified into categories: produce, dairy, bakery, and the like. And when we pursue a college major, we find the field of study divided into individual courses. Given the amount of information we must process every day, it would be difficult indeed to negotiate our way through life without classification and division. As a rhetorical strategy, classification and division allows writers to make sense of what might otherwise seem to be random ideas.

While the two strategies share similar principles, classification involves sorting items into categories, moving from the individual to the group, while division breaks a whole into parts, moving from group to individual. Thus, classification emphasizes similarities among items in a group, while division emphasizes differences. Such analyses allow us to understand how parts relate to wholes and how things work. In the supermarket, for example, products that share certain qualities are placed together: cheese, milk, cream, and butter can all be classified as dairy products. As a college major, the broad subject of American history is divided into courses that focus on different time periods: colonial, federal, Civil War, twentieth-century. Both classification and division help people to put information into a coherent order by identifying relationships either between parts and the whole or among parts.

For classification and division to be successful, the same *principle* must be used throughout the analysis. Think about how confusing it would be if the supermarket manager classified some products by *purpose*, some by *price*, and some by *brand*! There would be one aisle for dairy products, another for products over three dollars, and another for Kraft products. This failure to employ a uniform principle would result in some dairy products being in the dairy aisle, some in the over-three-dollar aisle, and some in the Kraft aisle. Shoppers would have an extremely difficult time finding their way around the store. Similarly, an essay dividing heads of state might use the categories of monarch, prime minister, and president. To also introduce male and female as categories would confuse the reader; no coherent order would emerge, because some of the categories are based on title and some on gender.

Maya Angelou uses classification and division to a limited extent in "Graduation." When she divides the general category academic honors, she uses a principle commonly used in elementary schools: "No absences, no tardiness, and my academic work was among the best of the year." And when she divides academic work into categories, she uses a performance principle more appropriate to a twelve year old: "I could say the preamble to the Constitution even faster than Bailey. . . . I had memorized the presidents of the United States from Washington to Roosevelt in chronological as well as alphabetical order."

In addition to ensuring that the same principle is used in classifying and dividing, it is also important to keep the *level* of the subclasses *parallel* and the treatment *equal*. Monarch, prime minister, and president, for example, are all parallel titles—each is a general category for a head of state. To introduce Ronald Reagan as a parallel category would not make sense; he represents a further subcategory, individual heads of state. Finally, the identification of categories should account for every significant item in the group: to neglect to include presidents as a class of heads of state would make for an incomplete treatment of the subject.

When Angelou classifies the opportunities open to children in the South in the 1940s, she creates two parallel classes: white children and African American children. She then creates several subclasses for each of the primary classes, treating each subclass equally: "The white kids were going to have a chance to become Galileos and Madame Curies and Edisons and Gaugins, and our boys (the girls weren't even in on it) would try to be Jesse Owenses and Joe Louises." The subclasses for white children include a variety of exalted occupations, including inventors, scientists, and painters; the subclasses for African American children are only two, both of them athletic: runners and boxers. That Angelou uses names of famous people keeps her classes equal; had she written, "inventors and women scientists and Gaugins," she would not have been treating the classes equally. And her limiting the classes open to African American children to only two accounts for what at that time constituted almost the only options open to those children.

As with other rhetorical strategies, classification and division must have a purpose. Dividing heads of state into subclasses allows a student of political science to examine different governmental systems; dividing a college major into separate courses allows a student to understand relationships among courses; classifying supermarket products into categories allows shoppers to find easily what they are looking for. Angelou's use of classification and division allows her readers to understand the mind of a twelve year old and to appreciate the limited options open to African American children as compared to white children in the 1940s. What matters is not whether the purpose is simple or profound; what matters is that there is a purpose.

Definition

Definition of terms and concepts is essential to the clear understanding of any subject. If the reader is to share common ground with the writer, then the writer has the responsibility to clarify his or her meaning to the reader. In some cases, definitions are *formal*: short, dictionary-like explanations of a term. If you were asked to define *psychoanalytic criticism*, for example, you might offer a brief definition: it is a school of criticism that relies on Freud's theories of personality development in analyzing literary works. Frequently, however, definitions are *extended*, requiring a paragraph, an essay, or even an entire book to clarify the meaning of a term or concept. If you were expected to apply psychoanalytic criticism to a novel, for example, you would need to explain the intricacies of the school, and this would require an extended definition. In this case, your entire essay might constitute an extended definition, with the novel serving as an example of this particular school of literary criticism.

Maya Angelou provides a brief definition of "A & M (agricultural and mechanical schools)" in "Graduation": they were schools "which trained Negro youths to be carpenters, farmers, handymen, masons, maids, cooks and baby nurses." When she is wallowing in the self-loathing brought on by Donleavy's speech, she engages in an extended definition of humanity, especially for African Americans:

> *It was awful to be a Negro and have no control over my life. It was brutal to be young and already trained to sit quietly and listen to charges brought against my color with no chance of defense. We should all be dead. I thought I should like to see us all dead, one on top of the other. A pyramid of flesh with the whitefolks on the bottom, as the broad base, then the Indians with their silly tomahawks and teepees and wigwams and treaties, the Negroes with their mops and recipes and cotton sacks and spirituals sticking out of their mouths. The Dutch children should all stumble in their wooden shoes and*

break their necks. The French should choke to death on the Louisiana Purchase (1803) while silkworms ate all the Chinese with their stupid pigtails. As a species, we were an abomination. All of us.

Both formal and extended definitions comprise three parts: *term*, *class*, and *differentiation*. The *term* is that which is being defined, psychoanalytic criticism, for example. The *class* identifies the general category in which the term is found—in this case, a school of literary criticism. *Differentiation* distinguishes the term from other terms in the same class, such as feminist criticism, formalist criticism, and Marxist criticism. If the definition is to be effective, all three parts must be clear, complete, and detailed. Depending on the audience, the language used in the definition can be either technical or general. An audience unfamiliar with Freud's theories, for example, would need to have the terms *id*, *ego*, and *superego* explained in lay terms, while an audience familiar with his work would be able to understand a technical explanation that assumed knowledge of these key terms. Although Angelou's extended definition of humanity is metaphorical rather than literal, it is still possible to identify term (races), class (humanity), and differentiation (whites, Indians, Negroes, Dutch, French, and Chinese).

Writers employing this rhetorical strategy must be careful to avoid what is known as *circular definition*, in which the term is simply restated in different words. For example, "Organic food is food that is grown organically" is a circular definition. The definition does *nothing* to help the reader understand the concept!

Using definition as a strategy can be interesting because it almost always involves other rhetorical strategies. Example is frequently used in defining terms: a song by the Mighty Mighty Bosstones, for example, might be used to help define *ska music*. Comparison and contrast might be used in the same definition, contrasting ska to heavy metal music. A definition of contemporary music in general might involve division and classification, dividing it into ska, rap, reggae, and other categories. In addition, a definition might use metaphor or analogy, comparing the term imaginatively to something else, or negation, stating what the term is not.

Angelou employs some of these strategies in "Graduation." She uses examples of African American working tools (mops, recipes, and cotton sacks) to help define her race. She contrasts the aspirations of white children and African American children to help define opportunity. And finally, she defines the human species by dividing it into different races.

Definition may be used for its own purpose, or it may support another purpose—*persuasion*, for example. Regardless of purpose, however, a good definition must be detailed, complete, and presented in such a way that the audience can understand it.

Example

If you have ever been asked to explain a theory or concept so that the average person can understand it, then you are aware of the importance of example. Examples are particularly useful in making abstractions concrete. A political scientist might offer the examples of Great Britain and Israel to explain the parliamentary system of government; a psychologist might offer the examples of particular patients to explain certain neuroses; a literary critic might offer the examples of Edith Wharton and Henry James to explain the concept of realism and naturalism. For examples like these to be effective, they must be relevant to the concept being explained. The examples must also be typical and not an exception; the concrete example must truly be representative of the concept.

In "Graduation," Maya Angelou presents the concept of segregation and racial discrimination through the example of Edward Donleavy's speech to the graduates, but within that example, she also provides specific examples of what segregation meant to her and her friends. When Donleavy sings the praises of African American athletes like Olympic star Jesse Owens and world heavyweight champion Joe Louis (known as the "Brown Bomber"), the young Angelou thinks,

> Owens and the Brown Bomber were great heroes in our world, but what school official in the white-goddom of Little Rock had the right to decide that those two men must be our only heroes? Who decided that for Henry Reed to become a scientist he had to work like George Washington Carver, as a bootblack, to buy a lousy microscope? Bailey was obviously always going to be too small to be an athlete, so which concrete angel glued to what country seat had decided that if my brother wanted to become a lawyer he had to first pay penance for his skin by picking cotton and hoeing corn and studying correspondence books at night for twenty years?

Angelou's examples of African Americans facing overwhelming obstacles in their quest for success are obvious to the reader. Not all examples are so obvious, however, and thus the writer who uses examples must be careful to explain or analyze how they relate to some concept. It is only when the example is as clearly relevant as Angelou's that the writer can leave it to the reader to figure out the connection.

As with other strategies of development, example requires that the writer use specific details in order to *show* rather than simply *tell*. Thus, Angelou uses names such as Jesse Owens, the Brown Bomber, and George Washington Carver; she also uses details such as the concrete angel glued to the country seat, as well as specific images of hoeing corn and picking cotton. All of these details help make the example clearer and more concrete in readers' minds. Example leaves the reader with a specific impression of the concept being explained; to that end, organization is crucial.

Sometimes a writer will use different examples to illustrate specific features of a concept. One patient, for example, might illustrate the idea that obsessive-compulsive disorder often interferes with an individual's capacity to perform at work, while another patient illustrates the impact of the disorder on family life. Or a writer may move from the least significant example to the most significant, and sometimes even from most to least significant. In Angelou's piece, the less important (to her) example of Henry Reed is presented first, with the more important example of her brother Bailey presented second—and in greater detail.

While example can be used as the primary rhetorical strategy of an essay, often it is used in support of other strategies. Writers of *argument* often use examples to provide *evidence* in support of a position, while writers of *definition* use examples to *clarify* the term being described. Often, a narrative is an extended example: "Graduation" might be considered, in its entirety, an example of the evils of segregation and the resilience of African Americans. Whatever the strategy, it is essential to remember that whether it is used as the primary or secondary strategy, example must always contribute to the specific point that the writer is trying to make.

Persuasion

Whenever you take a position on a subject and seek to convince others to join you, you are engaging in **persuasion**. Almost always linked with **argument**, persuasion is a strategy that employs not only the logic and reason of argument but appeals to emotion as well. Because most of the arguments you encounter involve both logical and emotional appeals, this discussion will use the term *persuasion* exclusively.

The purpose of persuasion can vary: Sometimes a writer seeks only to establish the validity of a particular position; sometimes a writer wishes to convince readers to change their minds on an issue; sometimes a writer is determined to commit readers to a specific course of action. For example, if you are involved in a movement to prevent the building of a toxic waste dump in your community, you may seek to persuade your audience in several ways. In addressing those who consider only the economic impact of the dump on the community, you simply may want to establish that the environmental position is valid and must be considered in any debate. You also may want to convince those who see no harm in the dump to recognize the impact on the air and water quality in the surrounding areas. And you may seek to convince those who agree that the dump is a hazard to take such actions as picketing the company building the dump, engaging in a letter-writing campaign to the local newspaper, or petitioning the company's stockholders to oppose the move.

What these examples also illustrate is that writers of persuasion must pay careful attention to their **audience**. If you are seeking, for example, to convince the environmentalists to take action against the dump, your appeal will be different from the one you would make to a group whose money is invested in the company building the dump. Some audiences will be entirely sympathetic to your position, some antithetic to it, and many will fall somewhere between those two extremes. Your task as a writer of persuasion is to appeal to the **beliefs** and **values** of your audience. If you can find common beliefs and values, your task will be that much easier. For example, most members of a community will be sensitive to the economic impact of a toxic waste dump; a facility providing both jobs and tax dollars is an attractive prospect. You will be more persuasive, then, if you can address economic concerns. Perhaps you might balance the economic advantages of a dump with the increased costs of health care, loss of work due to illness, and decline of property values in order to appeal to those whose position stems from their sense of economic values. (It is worth noting here that such an appeal would also incorporate the strategies of comparison and contrast and cause and effect. It is common for other rhetorical strategies to be used in support of persuasion.)

In a persuasive piece a writer usually supports rational appeals with appeals to emotion and to her integrity or credibility as well. These appeals derive from the Greek concept of **logic**, which highlights three factors essential to an effective argument: *logos* (soundness of argument), *pathos* (emotional power of language), and *ethos* (credibility or integrity of writer). Emotional appeals, if legitimately related to your position, will strengthen a purely rational argument. Maya Angelou uses emotional appeals effectively in "Graduation" when she describes how she felt after Edward Donleavy's speech:

> Graduation, the hush-hush magic time of frills and gifts and congratulations and diplomas, was finished for me before my name was called. The accomplishment was nothing. The meticulous maps, drawn in three colors of ink, learning and spelling decasyllabic words, memorizing the whole of *The Rape of Lucrece*—it was for nothing. Donleavy had exposed us.

The demoralization of a young girl whose hopes only recently had included heading "for the freedom of open fields" supports the implicit argument against segregation that permeates Angelou's piece. By allowing her audience to focus not on statistics and principles but rather on a real girl's disillusionment with her life and her race, she brings the issue into clearer focus for her readers by providing a personal touch.

"Graduation" also illustrates the significance of language to *pathos*. When considering the meaning of words, it is important to distinguish between *denotation*, the dictionary definition of the word, and *connotation*, the implied meaning or emotional overtones of the word. The word *group*, for example, is rather neutral in both denotation and connotation; it refers to a number of people with some common purpose. Change the word to *gang*, however, and while the dictionary meaning may remain essentially the same, the sinister implications of the word, the sense of danger or violence, cannot be ignored. Thus a newspaper account referring to a *group* of environmental activists creates a different image than one referring to a *gang* of activists. Angelou uses connotation when she asks why her brother has to "pay penance for his skin" in order to become a lawyer. Her reference to penance calls up religious images of sinning against God, thereby heightening the impact of this condemnation of segregation.

Angelou's *ethos* is established both within and without the essay. Within "Graduation" she establishes her credibility by clearly presenting herself as one who has suffered the inequities of segregation; she has first-hand experience of her subject. A brief look at Angelou's biography also establishes her *ethos*. Growing up in the segregated South and San Francisco, she overcame numerous obstacles to become the first black female conductor on the San Francisco cable cars, to excel as an accomplished writer and actor, and to be chosen to compose and present the ceremonial poem at President Bill Clinton's first inauguration. Her credentials lend credibility to her position. If you wish to establish your credibility and integrity in the fight against the toxic waste dump, you would have to make your understanding of the issues clear, highlight any education or professional experience relating to the issues, and present yourself as a reasonable, trustworthy person.

There is no better way to present yourself as reasonable and trustworthy than to **address opposing views** within your persuasive piece. Acknowledging the economic benefits of a toxic waste dump, for example, establishes you as a person who understands the validity of different points of view, thus enhancing your credibility. At the same time, **refuting** that argument with evidence of the economic costs of the dump strengthens your position.

In preparing a persuasive piece it is important to consider various approaches to argument and persuasion. Two of the more common approaches used today are the **Rogerian** and the **Toulmin** models. Using the Rogerian model, you would first acknowledge your opposition and assert its validity. This process would lead to finding a common ground from which all sides can view the issue. Finally, you would present evidence to establish your position as the most reasonable.

Another effective approach to argument and persuasion is found in the work of philosopher Stephen Toulmin, whose model stresses the importance of a strong link between the thesis of a persuasive piece and the evidence supporting that thesis. The primary parts of the Toulmin model are **claim** (thesis), **grounds** (evidence or emotional appeal), and **warrant** (assumption linking claim to grounds).

In using reason rather than emotional appeals in persuasion, it is necessary to understand the distinction between the two primary types of reasoning. **Inductive reasoning** involves moving from specific evidence to a general conclusion, while **deductive reasoning** moves from a general statement to specific conclusions. Using inductive reasoning to persuade your audience to oppose the toxic waste dump, for example, would be based on a collection of specific pieces of evidence:

Evidence:

Toxic waste dumps cause health problems.

Toxic waste dumps pose environmental dangers.

Toxic waste dumps result in lower property values.

Toxic waste dumps result in higher health-care costs.

Conclusion:

A toxic waste dump in this community should be opposed.

A deductive approach, on the other hand, would probably involve presenting a **syllogism**. A syllogism comprises three parts: the **major premise** (a general statement about a category or class), the **minor premise** (a specific statement about one member of that category or class), and the **conclusion** (derived about the specific member). If presented in the form of a syllogism, Maya Angelou's argument against segregation might look like this:

Major premise: Segregation is always unjust.

Minor premise: The school system of Stamps, Arkansas was segregated in the 1940s.

Conclusion: The school system of Stamps, Arkansas in the 1940s was unjust.

Looking at Angelou's piece in this way illustrates the interrelationship between rational arguments and emotional appeals. While the syllogism is valid, the real persuasive power of "Graduation" lies in the emotional response it engenders in readers. Similarly, the emotional appeal would lose its effectiveness if the rational argument were not valid.

It should be evident by now that persuasion is perhaps the most complex of the rhetorical strategies outlined here. The successful persuasive essay is directed at a specific audience, employs appropriate rational and emotional appeals, and follows the rules of logic.

On Keeping a Notebook

Joan Didion

Joan Didion (1934–) was born in Sacramento, Califor-nia. She received a B. A. at the University of California at Berkeley (1956), and then moved to New York City, where she spent seven years working as an associate editor at Vogue *and as a contributor to* Esquire, *the* National Re-view, *and the* Saturday Evening Post. *In 1964, Didion married writer John Gregory Dunne and returned to Cal-ifornia, where she began to write the essays and fiction that became her genre: personal commentaries on contemporary events that expose social disintegration. Her published works include the collections of essays* Slouching Towards Bethlehem *(1968),* The White Album *(1970), and* After Henry *(1992); the novels* Run River *(1963),* Play It As It Lays *(1970),* A Book of Common Prayer *(1977), and* Democracy *(1984); and the nonfiction books* Salvador *(1983),* Miami *(1987),* Political Fictions *(2001),* Where I Was From *(2003), and* The Year of Magical Thinking *(2005), for which she won the National Book Award for nonfiction. In this essay, Didion reveals that her writer's notebook, a real hodgepodge, is a necessary part of her being, but of symbolic value only to her.*

1   "'That woman Estelle,'" the note reads, "'is partly the reason why George Sharp and I are separated today.' *Dirty crépe-de-Chine wrap-per, hotel bar, Wilmington RR, 9:45 A.M. August Monday morning.*"

Since the note is in my notebook, it presumably has some mean-ing to me. I study it for a long while. At first I have only the most gen-eral notion of what I was doing on an August Monday morning in the bar of the hotel across from the Pennsylvania Railroad station in

From *Slouching Towards Bethlehem* by Joan Didion. Published by Farrar, Straus, Giroux, Inc. Copyright © 1961, 1967, 1968 by Joan Didion.

Wilmington, Delaware (waiting for a train? missing one? 1960? 1961? why Wilmington?), but I do remember being there. The woman in the dirty crêpe-de-Chine wrapper had come down from her room for a beer, and the bartender had heard before the reason why George Sharp and she were separated today. "Sure," he said, and went on mopping the floor. "You told me." At the other end of the bar is a girl. She is talking, pointedly, not to the man beside her but to a cat lying in the triangle of sunlight cast through the open door. She is wearing a plaid silk dress from Peck & Peck, and the hem is coming down.

Here is what it is: the girl has been on the Eastern Shore, and now she is going back to the city, leaving the man beside her, and all she can see ahead are the viscous summer sidewalks and the 3 A.M. long-distance calls that will make her lie awake and then sleep drugged through all the steaming mornings left in August (1960? 1961?). Because she must go directly from the train to lunch in New York, she wishes that she had a safety pin for the hem of the plaid silk dress, and she also wishes that she could forget about the hem and the lunch and stay in the cool bar that smells of disinfectant and malt and make friends with the woman in the crêpe-de-Chine wrapper. She is afflicted by a little self-pity, and she wants to compare Estelles. That is what that was all about.

Why did I write it down? In order to remember, of course, but exactly what was it I wanted to remember? How much of it actually happened? Did any of it? Why do I keep a notebook at all? It is easy to deceive oneself on all those scores. The impulse to write things down is a peculiarly compulsive one, inexplicable to those who do not share it, useful only accidentally, only secondarily, in the way that any compulsion tries to justify itself. I suppose that it begins or does not begin in the cradle. Although I have felt compelled to write things down since I was five years old, I doubt that my daughter ever will, for she is a singularly blessed and accepting child, delighted with life exactly as life presents itself to her, unafraid to go to sleep and unafraid to wake up. Keepers of private notebooks are a different breed altogether, lonely and resistant rearrangers of things, anxious malcontents, children afflicted apparently at birth with some presentiment of loss.

My first notebook was a Big Five tablet, given to me by my mother with the sensible suggestion that I stop whining and learn to amuse myself by writing down my thoughts. She returned the tablet to me a few years ago; the first entry is an account of a woman who believed herself to be freezing to death in the Arctic night, only to find, when day broke, that she had stumbled onto the Sahara Desert, where she would die of the heat before lunch. I have no idea what turn of a five-year-old's mind could have prompted so insistently "ironic" and exotic a story, but it does reveal a certain predilection for the extreme which has dogged me into adult life; perhaps if I were analytically inclined I would find it a truer story than any I might have told about Donald Johnson's birthday party or the day my cousin Brenda put Kitty Litter in the aquarium.

So the point of my keeping a notebook has never been, nor is it now, to have an accurate factual record of what I have been doing or thinking. That would be a different impulse entirely, an instinct for reality which I sometimes envy but do not possess. At no point have I ever been able successfully to keep a diary; my approach to daily life ranges from the grossly negligent to the merely absent, and on those few occasions when I have tried dutifully to record a day's events, boredom has so overcome me that the results are mysterious at best. What is this business about "shopping, typing piece, dinner with E, depressed"? Shopping for what? Type what piece? Who is E? Was this "E" depressed, or was I depressed? Who cares?

In fact I have abandoned altogether that kind of pointless entry; instead I tell what some would call lies. "That's simply not true," the members of my family frequently tell me when they come up against my memory of a shared event. "The party was not for you, the spider was *not* a black widow, *it wasn't that way at all.*" Very likely they are right, for not only have I always had trouble distinguishing between what happened and what merely might have happened, but I remain unconvinced that the distinction, for my purposes, matters. The cracked crab that I recall having for lunch the day my father came home from Detroit in 1945 must certainly be embroidery, worked into the day's pattern to lend verisimilitude; I was ten years old and would not now remember the cracked crab. The day's events did not turn on cracked crab. And yet it is precisely that fictitious crab that makes me see the afternoon all over again, a home movie run all too often, the father bearing gifts, the child weeping, an exercise in family love and guilt. Or that is what it was to me. Similarly, perhaps it never did snow that August in Vermont; perhaps there never were flurries in the night wind, and maybe no one else felt the ground hardening and summer already dead even as we pretended to bask in it, but that was how it felt to me; and it might as well have snowed, could have snowed, did snow.

How it felt to me: that is getting closer to the truth about a note-book. I sometimes delude myself about why I keep a notebook, imagine that some thrifty virtue derives from preserving everything observed. See enough and write it down, I tell myself and then some morning when the world seems drained of wonder, some day when I am only going through the motions of doing what I am supposed to do, which is write—on that bankrupt morning I will simply open my notebook and there it will be, a forgotten account with accumulated interest, paid passage back to the world out there: dialogue overheard in hotels and elevators and at the hatcheck counter in Pavillon (one middle-aged man shows his hat check to another and says, "That's my old football number"); impressions of Bettina Aptheker and Benjamin Sonnenberg and Teddy ("Mr. Acapulco") Stauffer; careful *aperçus* about tennis bums and failed fashion models and Greek shipping heiresses, one of whom taught me a significant lesson (a lesson I could have learned from F. Scott Fitzgerald, but perhaps we all must meet the very rich for ourselves) by asking, when I arrived to interview her in her orchid-filled sitting room on the second day of a paralyzing New York blizzard, whether it was snowing outside.

I imagine, in other words, that the notebook is about other people. But of course it is not. I have no real business with what one stranger said to another at the hatcheck counter in Pavillon; in fact I suspect that the line "That's my old football number" touched not my own imagination at all, but merely some memory of something once read, probably "The Eighty-Yard Run." Nor is my concern with a woman in a dirty crépe-de-Chine wrapper in a Wilmington bar. My stake is always, of course, in the unmentioned girl in the plaid silk dress. *Remember what it was to be me:* that is always the point.

It is a difficult point to admit. We are brought up in the ethic that others, any others, all others, are by definition more interesting than ourselves; taught to be diffident, just this side of self-effacing. ("You're the least important person in the room and don't forget it," Jessica Mitford's governess would hiss in her ear on the advent of any social occasion; I copied that into my notebook because it is only recently that I have been able to enter a room without hearing some such phrase in my inner ear.) Only the very young and the very old may recount their dreams at breakfast, dwell upon self, interrupt with memories of beach picnics and favorite Liberty lawn dresses and the rainbow trout in a creek near Colorado Springs. The rest of us are expected, rightly, to affect absorption in other people's favorite dresses, other people's trout.

And so we do. But our notebooks give us away, for however dutifully we record what we see around us, the common denominator of all we see is always, transparently, shamelessly, the implacable "I." We are not talking here about the kind of notebook that is patently for public consumption, a structural conceit for binding together a series of graceful *pensées;* we are talking about something private, about bits of the mind's string too short to use, an indiscriminate and erratic assemblage with meaning only for its maker.

And sometimes even the maker has difficulty with the meaning. There does not seem to be, for example, any point in my knowing for the rest of my life that, during 1964, 720 tons of soot fell on every square mile of New York City, yet there it is in my notebook, labeled "FACT." Nor do I really need to remember that Ambrose Bierce liked to spell Leland Stanford's name "£eland $tanford" or that "smart women almost always wear black in Cuba," a fashion hint without much potential for practical application. And does not the relevance of these notes seem marginal at best?:

> In the basement of the Inyo County Courthouse in Independence, California, sign pinned to a mandarin coat: "This MANDARIN COAT was often worn by Mrs. Minnie S. Brooks when giving lectures on her TEAPOT COLLECTION." Redhead getting out of car in front of Beverly Wilshire Hotel, chinchilla stole, Vuitton bags with tags reading:
> MRS LOU FOX
> HOTEL SAHARA
> VEGAS

Well, perhaps not entirely marginal. As a matter of fact, Mrs. Minnie S. Brooks and her MANDARIN COAT pull me back into my own childhood, for although I never knew Mrs. Brooks and did not visit Inyo County until I was thirty, I grew up in just such a world, in houses cluttered with Indian relics and bits of gold ore and ambergris and the souvenirs my Aunt Mercy Farnsworth brought back from the Orient. It is a long way from that world to Mrs. Lou Fox's world where we all live now, and is it not just as well to remember that? Might not

Mrs. Minnie S. Brooks help me to remember what I am? Might not Mrs. Lou Fox help me to remember what I am not?

But sometimes the point is harder to discern. What exactly did I have in mind when I noted down that it cost the father of someone I know $650 a month to light the place on the Hudson in which he lived before the Crash? What use was I planning to make of this line by Jimmy Hoffa: "I may have my faults, but being wrong ain't one of them"? And although I think it interesting to know where the girls who travel with the Syndicate have their hair done when they find themselves on the West Coast, will I ever make suitable use of it? Might I not be better off just passing it on to John O'Hara? What is a recipe for sauerkraut doing in my notebook? What kind of magpie keeps this notebook? "*He was born the night the* Titanic *went down.*" That seems a nice enough line, and I even recall who said it, but is it not really a better line in life than it could ever be in fiction?

But of course that is exactly it: not that I should ever use the line, but that I should remember the woman who said it and the afternoon I heard it. We were on her terrace by the sea, and we were finishing the wine left from lunch, trying to get what sun there was, a California winter sun. The woman whose husband was born the night the *Titanic* went down wanted to rent her house, wanted to go back to her children in Paris. I remember wishing that I could afford the house, which cost $1,000 a month. "Someday you will," she said lazily. "Someday it all comes." There in the sun on her terrace it seemed easy to believe in someday but later I had a low-grade afternoon hangover and ran over a black snake on the way to the supermarket and was flooded with inexplicable fear when I heard the checkout clerk explaining to the man ahead of me why she was finally divorcing her husband. "He left me no choice," she said over and over as she punched the register. "He has a little seven-month-old baby by her, he left me no choice." I would like to believe that my dread then was for the human condition, but of course it was for me, because I wanted a baby and did not then have one and because I wanted to own the house that cost $1,000 a month to rent and because I had a hangover.

It all comes back. Perhaps it is difficult to see the value in having one's self back in that kind of mood, but I do see it; I think we are well advised to keep on nodding terms with the people we used to be, whether we find them attractive company or not. Otherwise they turn up unannounced and surprise us, come hammering on the mind's door at 4 A.M. of a bad night and demand to know who deserted them, who betrayed them, who is going to make amends. We forget all too soon the things we thought we could never forget. We forget the loves and the betrayals alike, forget what we whispered and what we screamed, forget who we were. I have already lost touch with a couple of people I used to be; one of them, a seventeen-year-old, presents little threat, although it would be of some interest to me to know again what it feels like to sit on a river levee drinking vodka-and-orange-juice and listening to Les Paul and Mary Ford and their echoes sing "How High the Moon" on the car radio. (You see I still have the scenes, but I no longer perceive myself among those present, no longer could even improvise the dialogue.) The other one, a twenty-three-year-old, bothers me more. She was always a good deal of trouble, and I suspect she will reappear when I least want to see her, skirts too long, shy to the point of aggravation, always the injured party, full of recriminations and little hurts and stories I do not want to hear again, at once saddening me and angering me with her vulnerability and ignorance, an apparition all the more insistent for being so long banished.

It is a good idea, then, to keep in touch and I suppose that keeping in touch is what notebooks are all about. And we are all on our own when it comes to keeping those lines open to ourselves: your notebooks will never help me, nor mine you. "*So what's new in the whiskey business?*" What could that possibly mean to you? To me it means a blonde in a Pucci bathing suit sitting with a couple of fat men by the pool at the Beverly Hills Hotel. Another man approaches, and they all regard one another in silence for a while. "So what's new in the whiskey business?" one of the fat men finally says by way of welcome, and the blonde stands up, arches one foot and dips it in the pool, looking all the while at the cabana where Baby Pignatari is talking on the telephone. That is all there is to that, except that several years later I saw the blonde coming out of Saks Fifth Avenue in New York with her California complexion and a voluminous mink coat. In the harsh wind that day she looked old and irrevocably tired to me, and even the skins in the mink coat were not worked the way they were doing them that year, not the way she would have wanted them done, and there is the point of the story. For a while after that I did not like to look in the mirror, and my eyes would skim the newspapers and pick out only the deaths, the cancer victims, the premature coronaries, the suicides, and I stopped riding the Lexington Avenue IRT because I noticed for the first time that all the strangers I had seen for years—the man with the seeing-eye dog, the spinster who read the classified pages every day, the fat girl who always got off with me at Grand Central—looked older than they once had.

It all comes back. Even that recipe for sauerkraut: even that brings it back. I was on Fire Island when I first made sauerkraut, and it was raining, and we drank a lot of bourbon and ate the sauerkraut and went to bed at ten, and I listened to the rain and the Atlantic and felt safe. I made the sauerkraut again last night and it did not make me feel any safer, but that is, as they say, another story.

Questions on Meaning

1. Didion provides a number of reasons why she believes it is a good idea to keep a notebook. Without looking at her essay, write as many reasons for keeping a notebook as you can recall, and then reread the essay and check your answers. Note that Didion sometimes states what are *not* good reasons for keeping a notebook.
2. Why does Didion say that a personal notebook has "meaning only for its maker," that "your notebooks will never help me, nor mine you"?
3. What do Didion's notebooks tell her about herself? Why does she feel it is important "to keep in touch" with who she used to be? Why is it not always pleasing to her to make contact with her past?
4. What is the role of the anecdotal stories Didion relates as she describes her notebooks and her reasons for keeping notebooks? How would it affect the essay to remove these narrative segments?

Questions on Rhetorical Strategy and Style

1. Describe the main rhetorical strategies Didion uses in this essay. Scan the essay, marking passages that represent these different strategies.
2. Didion asks rhetorical questions throughout this essay. Sometimes she answers them, sometimes not. What is the effect of this writing style? Choose two or three of these questions and try to rewrite them as declarative statements. How do your revised sentences change the meaning of the passages?

Writing Assignments

1. Find something you have written that would have no value to someone else—class notes, a shopping list, directions to a party, or a personal notebook. Reread your notes. Have they retained their meaning? What do they say about what was going on at the time you wrote them? What do they say about *you*?
2. As Didion indicates, a diary and a personal notebook are vastly different. To explore the differences between these types of journals, write both a diary description and a *personal notebook* description of one day this week. In the diary record for yourself

what happened on that day. In the personal notebook, record your impressions, reactions, and ruminations, and explain "how it felt to me." Compare and contrast your diary to your personal journal. Consider what each would mean to someone else; consider what each says about *you.*

3. Write an essay about something you do that is personal, something you don't share with anyone else, something that few people would understand. It might be a secret place you go to think, or poetry or drawings that only you see, or an Eastern religion that you are studying. Describe why you keep it private. Explain why it would be of little value to others. Explore what it says about *you.*

Texts

Ursula K. Le Guin

Born in 1929 in Berkeley, California, Ursula K. Le Guin is one of America's most prolific and versatile writers, although particularly noted for her works of fantasy and science fiction. She was raised in an academic family. Her father was a well-known anthropologist and her mother was the author of an influential book on the Yana Indians. Le Guin's list of awards is commanding. She has won the National Book Award and a Newberry Honor. Also, she has won the Hugo and Nebula Awards numerous times, solidifying her place as perhaps the most acknowledged writer of fantasy and science fiction. A few of her most recent works are Sixty Odd: New Poems *(1999),* Tao Te Ching: A Book About the Way and the Power of the Way *(1997),* The Twins, the Dream: Two Voices *(1996), and* Unlocking the Air and Other Stories *(1996). The following selection is from* Searoad: Chronicles of Klatsand *(1990). It tells the story of a woman who attempts to understand the language of the sea.*

1   Messages came, Johanna thought, usually years too late, or years before one could crack their code or had even learned the language they were in. Yet they came increasingly often and were so urgent, so compelling in their demand that she read them, that she do something, as to force her at last to take refuge from them. She rented, for the month of January, a little house with no telephone in a seaside town that had no mail delivery. She had stayed there several times in summer; winter, as she had hoped, was even quieter than summer. A whole day would go by without her hearing or speaking a

"Texts," by Ursula Le Guin, reprinted from *Searoad: Chronicles of Klatsand,* 1991, HarperCollins. Reprinted with permission by Virginia Kidd Agency, Inc.

word. She did not buy the paper or turn on the television, and the one morning she thought she ought to find some news on the radio she got a program in Finnish from Astoria. But the messages still came. Words were everywhere.

Literate clothing was no real problem. She remembered the first print dress she had ever seen, years ago, a genuine *print* dress with typography involved in the design—green on white, suitcases and hibiscus and the names *Riviera* and *Capri* and *Paris* occurring rather blobbily from shoulder-seam to hem, sometimes right side up, sometimes upside down. Then it had been, as the saleswoman said, very unusual. Now it was hard to find a T-shirt that did not urge political action, or quote lengthily from a dead physicist, or at least mention the town it was for sale in. All this she had coped with, she had even worn. But too many things were becoming legible.

She had noticed in earlier years that the lines of foam left by waves on the sand after stormy weather lay sometimes in curves that looked like handwriting, cursive lines broken by spaces, as if in words; but it was not until she had been alone for over a fortnight and had walked many times down to Wreck Point and back that she found she could read the writing. It was a mild day, nearly windless, so that she did not have to march briskly but could mosey along between the foam-lines and water's edge where the sand reflected the sky. Every now and then a quiet winter breaker driving up and up the beach would drive her and a few gulls ahead of it onto the drier sand; then as the wave receded she and the gulls would follow it back. There was not another soul on the long beach. The sand lay as firm and even as a pad of pale brown paper, and on it a recent wave at its high mark had left a complicated series of curves and bits of foam. The ribbons and loops and lengths of white looked so much like handwriting in chalk that she stopped, the way she would stop, half willingly, to read what people scratched in the sand in summer. Usually it was "Jason+Karen" or paired initials in a heart; once, mysteriously and memorably, three initials and the dates 1973–1984, the only such inscription that spoke of a promise not made but broken. Whatever those eleven years had been, the length of a marriage? a child's life? they were gone, and the letters and numbers also were gone when she came back by where they had been, with the tide rising. She had wondered then if the person who wrote them had written them to be erased. But these foam words lying on the brown sand now had been written by the erasing sea itself. If she could read them they might tell her a wisdom a good deal deeper and bitterer than she could possibly swallow. Do I want to know what the sea writes? she thought, but at the same time she was already reading the foam, which though in vaguely cuneiform blobs rather than letters of any alphabet was perfectly legible as she walked along beside it. "Yes," it read, "esse hes hetu tokye to' ossusess ekyes. Seham hute' u." (When she wrote it down later she used the apostrophe to represent a kind of stop or click like the last sound in "Yep!") As she read it over, backing up some yards to do so, it continued to say the same thing, so she walked up and down it several times and memorised it. Presently, as bubbles burst and the blobs began to shrink, it changed here and there to read, "Yes, e hes etu kye to' ossusess kye. ham te u." She felt that this was not significant change but mere loss, and kept the original text in mind. The water of the foam sank into the sand and the bubbles dried away till the marks and lines lessened into a faint lacework of dots and scraps, half legible. It looked enough like delicate bits of fancywork that she wondered if one could also read lace or crochet.

When she got home she wrote down the foam words so that she would not have to keep repeating them to remember them, and then she looked at the machine-made Quaker lace tablecloth on the little round dining table. It was not hard to read but was, as one might expect, rather dull. She made out the first line inside the border as "pith wot pith wot pith wot" interminably, with a "dub" every thirty stitches where the border pattern interrupted.

But the lace collar she had picked up at a second-hand clothes store in Portland was a different matter entirely. It was handmade, hand written. The script was small and very even. Like the Spencerian hand she had been taught fifty years ago in the first grade, it was ornate but surprisingly easy to read. "My soul must go," was the border, repeated many times, "My soul must go, my soul must go," and the fragile webs leading inward read, "sister, sister, sister, light the light." And she did not know what she was to do, or how she was to do it.

Questions on Meaning

1. What sort of texts do you find in this short piece? What is the significance of reading the things the protagonist attempts to decipher?
2. What is the significance of the opening passage, and the closing passage? What is their relationship?
3. Why is the woman in this story so compelled by the language she finds in places?

Questions on Rhetorical Strategy and Style

1. This story is written solely from the point of view of one character. What effect is achieved by this strategy? How does it add to our understanding of the character?
2. Examine the descriptive language in the story. What does that language tell us about the woman that we must understand to appreciate consciousness?

Writing Assignments

1. Write an essay in which you discuss the story as one person's journey toward an understanding of life's meaning. Talk about mysteries you have encountered in your own life and how you have come to terms with them.
2. Write an essay about an experience with nature that changed your view of things. Be descriptive in such a way that your readers may understand your relationship to the place and its significance to you.

Grant and Lee: A Study in Contrasts

Bruce Catton

Bruce Catton (1899–1978) is best known for his popular histories of the American Civil War. He wrote a dozen books and many articles about the War, including A Stillness at Appomattox, which won the Pulitzer Prize and the National Book Award in 1954. Having first worked as a newspaper journalist, Catton was interested in writing for the popular press rather than scholarly historians, and his writing always sought to make history real and living. "Grant and Lee: A Study in Contrasts" was published in 1956 in a book of essays by various historians called The American Story. *As you read it, notice how Catton takes us far beyond just the story of these two Civil War generals meeting at the end of the War—he is indeed writing a chapter in an American story. As you read this focused exploration of the character of these two men and the times they embody, you will also be learning something about the Civil War itself and the nature of great men.*

1   When Ulysses S. Grant and Robert E. Lee met in the parlor of a modest house at Appomattox Court House, Virginia, on April 9, 1865, to work out the terms for the surrender of Lee's Army of Northern Virginia, a great chapter in American life came to a close, and a great new chapter began.

These men were bringing the Civil War to its virtual finish. To be sure, other armies had yet to surrender, and for a few days the fugitive Confederate government would struggle desperately and vainly, trying to find some way to go on living now that its chief support was gone.

From *The American Story,* edited by Earl Schenck Miers. Published by the U.S. Capitol Historical Society.

But in effect it was all over when Grant and Lee signed the papers. And the little room where they wrote out the terms was the scene of one of the poignant, dramatic contrasts in American history.

They were two strong men, these oddly different generals, and they represented the strengths of two conflicting currents that, through them, had come into final collision.

Back of Robert E. Lee was the notion that the old aristocratic concept might somehow survive and be dominant in American life.

5   Lee was tidewater Virginia, and in his background were family,   5
culture, and tradition . . . the age of chivalry transplanted to a New World which was making its own legends and its own myths. He embodied a way of life that had come down through the age of knighthood and the English country squire. America was a land that was beginning all over again, dedicated to nothing much more complicated than the rather hazy belief that all men had equal rights and should have an equal chance in the world. In such a land Lee stood for the feeling that it was somehow of advantage to human society to have a pronounced inequality in the social structure. There should be a leisure class, backed by ownership of land; in turn, society itself should be keyed to the land as the chief source of wealth and influence. It would bring forth (according to this ideal) a class of men with a strong sense of obligation to the community; men who lived not to gain advantage for themselves, but to meet the solemn obligations which had been laid on them by the very fact that they were privileged. From them the country would get its leadership; to them it could look for the higher values—of thought, of conduct, of personal deportment—to give it strength and virtue. ·

Lee embodied the noblest elements of this aristocratic ideal. Through him, the landed nobility justified itself. For four years, the Southern states had fought a desperate war to uphold the ideals for which Lee stood. In the end, it almost seemed as if the Confederacy fought for Lee; as if he himself was the Confederacy . . . the best thing that the way of life for which the Confederacy stood could ever have to offer. He had passed into legend before Appomattox. Thousands of tired, underfed, poorly clothed Confederate soldiers, long since past the simple enthusiasm of the early days of the struggle, somehow considered Lee the symbol of everything for which they had been willing to die. But they could not quite put this feeling into words. If the Lost Cause, sanctified by so much heroism and so many deaths, had a living justification, its justification was General Lee.

Grant, the son of a tanner on the Western frontier, was everything Lee was not. He had come up the hard way and embodied nothing in particular except the eternal toughness and sinewy fiber of the men who grew up beyond the mountains. He was one of a body of men who owed reverence and obeisance to no one, who were self-reliant to a fault, who cared hardly anything for the past but who had a sharp eye for the future.

These frontier men were the precise opposites of the tidewater aristocrats. Back of them, in the great surge that had taken people over the Alleghenies and into the opening Western country, there was a deep, implicit dissatisfaction with a past that had settled into grooves. They stood for democracy, not from any reasoned conclusion about the proper ordering of human society, but simply because they had grown up in the middle of democracy and knew how it worked. Their society might have privileges, but they would be privileges each man had won for himself. Forms and patterns meant nothing. No man was born to anything, except perhaps to a chance to show how far he could rise. Life was competition.

Yet along with this feeling had come a deep sense of belonging to a national community. The Westerner who developed a farm, opened a shop, or set up in business as a trader, could hope to prosper only as his own community prospered—and his community ran from the Atlantic to the Pacific and from Canada down to Mexico. If the land was settled, with towns and highways and accessible markets, he could better himself. He saw his fate in terms of the nation's own destiny. As its horizons expanded, so did his. He had, in other words, an acute dollars-and-cents stake in the continued growth and development of his country.

10 And that, perhaps, is where the contrast between Grant and Lee 10 becomes most striking. The Virginia aristocrat, inevitably, saw himself in relation to his own region. He lived in a static society which could endure almost anything except change. Instinctively, his first loyalty would go to the locality in which that society existed. He would fight to the limit of endurance to defend it, because in defending it he was defending everything that gave his own life its deepest meaning.

The Westerner, on the other hand, would fight with an equal tenacity for the broader concept of society. He fought so because everything he lived by was tied to growth, expansion, and a constantly widening horizon. What he lived by would survive or fall with the nation itself. He could not possibly stand by unmoved in the face of an attempt to destroy the Union. He would combat it with everything he had, because he could only see it as an effort to cut the ground out from under his feet.

So Grant and Lee were in complete contrast, representing two diametrically opposed elements in American life. Grant was the modern man emerging; beyond him, ready to come on the stage, was the great age of steel and machinery, of crowded cities and a restless burgeoning vitality. Lee might have ridden down from the old age of chivalry, lance in hand, silken banner fluttering over his head. Each man was the perfect champion of his cause, drawing both his strengths and his weaknesses from the people he led.

Yet it was not all contrast, after all. Different as they were—in background, in personality, in underlying aspiration—these two great soldiers had much in common. Under everything else, they were marvelous fighters. Furthermore, their fighting qualities were really very much alike.

Each man had, to begin with, the great virtue of utter tenacity and fidelity. Grant fought his way down the Mississippi Valley in spite of acute personal discouragement and profound military handicaps. Lee hung on in the trenches at Petersburg after hope itself had died. In each man there was an indomitable quality . . . the born fighter's refusal to give up as long as he can still remain on his feet and lift his two fists.

15 Daring and resourcefulness they had, too; the ability to think 15 faster and move faster than the enemy. These were the qualities which gave Lee the dazzling campaigns of Second Manassas and Chancellorsville and won Vicksburg for Grant.

Lastly, and perhaps greatest of all, there was the ability, at the end, to turn quickly from war to peace once the fighting was over. Out of the way these two men behaved at Appomattox came the possibility of a peace of reconciliation. It was a possibility not wholly realized, in the years to come, but which did, in the end, help the two sections to become one nation again . . . after a war whose bitterness might have seemed to make such a reunion wholly impossible. No part of either man's life became him more than the part he played in this brief meeting in the McLean house at Appomattox. Their behavior there put all succeeding generations of Americans in their debt. Two great Americans, Grant and Lee—very different, yet under everything very much alike. Their encounter at Appomattox was one of the great moments of American history.

Questions on Meaning

1. As you read the essay, did you sense that Catton respected either Grant or Lee more than the other? If so, go back through the essay and underline phrases and sentences that give this impression. If not, explain how he manages to maintain such even-handedness while describing contrasting figures.
2. How has your understanding of these men, or the Civil War in general, been changed after reading this essay?
3. Catton speaks of Grant and Lee as "representing two diametrically opposed elements in American life." Without looking back to the essay, summarize these two aspects of America. Do you see any parallels to these two aspects in contemporary America?

Questions on Rhetorical Strategy and Style

1. Catton obviously uses the rhetorical strategies of comparison and contrast to shape the essay and develop its themes. Examining one paragraph at a time, make a brief outline of the essay that shows how Catton balances and finally integrates his exploration of the two men.
2. Like most effective writers arguing his ideas, Catton supports and develops his generalizations with examples—even in this brief, general essay. Reread the essay and take note of how specifics are used to demonstrate the abstract character traits Catton describes, such as these generals' "utter tenacity."
3. The essay's title emphasizes differences between Grant and Lee, as does the opening statement about "one of the poignant, dramatic contrasts in American history." Other phrases throughout the essay, such as "precise opposites," further this contrast. Yet by the end of the essay we see Grant and Lee have become "very much alike." How has the war brought about these changes in the two generals' characters?

Writing Assignments

1. As a historian, Catton is interested in broad sweeping changes in a society or culture as well as the individual stories of individual people. When he ends this essay with the statement about "one of the great moments in American history," we see again that the essay is about a much larger change in America. Choose a

different "moment" in U.S. or world history that you think represents a significant change from one time to another. Write an essay explaining that change.

2. Choose two people you admire: one a public figure, the other someone you have known personally. Write an essay in which you explore the admirable characteristics of both, looking for both similarities and differences.

That Lean and Hungry Look

Suzanne Britt Jordan

Suzanne Britt Jordan was born in Winston-Salem, North Carolina. Educated at Salem College and Washington University, where she received an M.A. in English, she has taught English at Meredith College. Widely published, Jordan has written columns for North Carolina Gardens & Homes *and the* Dickens Dispatch *(a national newsletter for Charles Dickens devotees) and articles for the* Baltimore Sun, Books and Religion, *the* Boston Globe, Long Island Newsday, The New York Times, *and* Newsweek. *Her essays have been collected in* Skinny People Are Dull and Crunchy Like Carrots *(1982) and* Show and Tell *(1983). She has also published a history of Meredith College and two English textbooks. This essay, which appeared in* Newsweek *and in* Skinny People, *exhibits her casual yet perceptive writing style. As she touts the qualities of fat over thin, judge yourself, as Jordan might judge you!*

1   Caesar was right. Thin people need watching. I've been watching them for most of my adult life, and I don't like what I see. When these narrow fellows spring at me, I quiver to my toes. Thin people come in all personalities, most of them menacing. You've got your "together" thin person, your mechanical thin person, your condescending thin person, your tsk-tsk thin person, your efficiency-expert thin person. All of them are dangerous.

In the first place, thin people aren't fun. They don't know how to goof off, at least in the best, fat sense of the word. They've always got to be adoing. Give them a coffee break, and they'll jog around the block. Supply them with a quiet evening at home, and they'll fix the

---

screen door and lick S&H green stamps. They say things like "there aren't enough hours in the day." Fat people never say that. Fat people think the day is too damn long already.

Thin people make me tired. They've got speedy little metabolisms that cause them to bustle briskly. They're forever rubbing their bony hands together and eyeing new problems to "tackle." I like to surround myself with sluggish, inert, easygoing fat people, the kind who believe that if you clean it up today, it'll just get dirty again tomorrow.

Some people say the business about the jolly fat person is a myth, that all of us chubbies are neurotic, sick, sad people. I disagree. Fat people may not be chortling all day long, but they're a hell of a lot *nicer* than the wizened and shriveled. Thin people turn surly, mean, and hard at a young age because they never learn the value of a hot-fudge sundae for easing tension. Thin people don't like gooey soft things because they themselves are neither gooey nor soft. They are crunchy and dull, like carrots. They go straight to the heart of the matter while fat people let things stay all blurry and hazy and vague, the way things actually are. Thin people want to face the truth. Fat people know there is no truth. One of my thin friends is always staring at complex, unsolvable problems and saying, "The key thing is. . . ." Fat people never say that. They know there isn't any such thing as the key thing about anything.

5 Thin people believe in logic. Fat people see all sides. The sides fat people see are rounded blobs, usually gray, always nebulous and truly not worth worrying about. But the thin person persists. "If you consume more calories than you burn," says one of my thin friends, "you will gain weight. It's that simple." Fat people always grin when they hear statements like that. They know better.

Fat people realize that life is illogical and unfair. They know very well that God is not in his heaven and all is not right with the world. If God is up there, fat people could have two doughnuts and a big orange drink anytime they wanted it.

Thin people have a long list of logical things they are always spouting off to me. They hold up one finger at a time as they reel off these things, so I won't lose track. They speak slowly as if to a young child. The list is long and full of holes. It contains tidbits like "get a grip on yourself," "cigarettes kill," "cholesterol clogs," "fit as a fiddle," "ducks in a row," "organize," and "sound fiscal management." Phrases like that.

They think these 2,000-point plans lead to happiness. Fat people know happiness is elusive at best and even if they could get the kind thin people talk about, they wouldn't want it. Wisely, fat people see that such programs are too dull, too hard, too off the mark. They are never better than a whole cheesecake.

Fat people know all about the mystery of life. They are the ones acquainted with the night, with luck, with fate, with playing it by ear. One thin person I know once suggested that we arrange all the parts of a jigsaw puzzle into groups according to size, shape, and color. He figured this would cut the time needed to complete the puzzle by at least 50 percent. I said I wouldn't do it. One, I like to muddle through. Two, what good would it do to finish early? Three, the jigsaw puzzle isn't the important thing. The important thing is the fun of four peo- 10 ple (one thin person included) sitting around a card table, working a jigsaw puzzle. My thin friend had no use for my list. Instead of join- 10 ing us, he went outside and mulched the boxwoods. The three re- maining fat people finished the puzzle and made chocolate, double-fudged brownies to celebrate.

10   The main problem with thin people is they oppress. Their good intentions, bony torsos, tight ships, neat corners, cerebral machina- tions, and pat solutions loom like dark clouds over the loose, com- fortable, spread-out, soft world of the fat. Long after fat people have removed their coats and shoes and put their feet up on the coffee table, thin people are still sitting on the edge of the sofa, looking neat as a pin, discussing rutabagas. Fat people are heavily into fits of laughter, slapping their thighs and whooping it up, while thin people are still politely waiting for the punch line.

Thin people are downers. They like math and morality and rea- soned evaluation of the limitations of human beings. They have their skinny little acts together. They expound, prognose, probe, and prick.

Fat people are convivial. They will like you even if you're irregu- lar and have acne. They will come up with a good reason why you never wrote the great American novel. They will cry in your beer with you. They will put your name in the pot. They will let you off the hook. Fat people will gab, giggle, guffaw, galumph, gyrate, and gossip. They are generous, giving, and gallant. They are gluttonous and goodly and great. What you want when you're down is soft and jiggly, not muscled and stable. Fat people know this. Fat people have plenty of room. Fat people will take you in.

Questions on Meaning

1. In your own words, what is Jordan's thesis? Identify the sentence that most closely expresses the thesis of the essay.
2. What does Jordan mean by the made-up word "adoing" in the second paragraph? What can you infer from the sound of the word and the tone of the sentence in which it is used?
3. What are Jordan's three reasons for not working efficiently on a jigsaw puzzle? How do those reasons reflect her approach to other aspects of life?

Questions on Rhetorical Strategy and Style

1. Identify how Jordan compares and contrasts fat and thin people in regard to their free time, their humor, their logic, and their view of the mysteries of life.
2. Jordan has filled her essay with aphorisms, such as "there isn't any such thing as the key thing about anything" and "life is illogical and unfair." Find two other aphorisms. What effect do these expressions have? How do they reflect her image of fat people?
3. Reread the last sentence of both the opening and closing paragraphs. How has Jordan linked those paragraphs? How do these paragraphs reflect the thesis of the essay?

Writing Assignments

1. In presenting her argument, Jordan employs satire, exaggeration, and some gross generalizations. How do they apply to you and your friends? Compare and contrast the fat and thin people you know with the characteristics Jordan outlines.
2. In many ways, the fat person described by Jordan represents a different time when folks weren't so rushed. Write an essay describing your pace of life. Compare and contrast your pace of life with that of your closest two or three friends. How would you like to change your lifestyle? Explain why you would or would not want to return to a time when life was slower and simpler.

Why We Crave Horror Movies

Stephen King

Stephen King (1947 –) was born in Portland, Maine. After graduating from the University of Maine in 1970, King held a number of jobs—knitting mill worker, janitor, high school English teacher—before gaining fame and fortune as a mystery writer. A prolific and widely popular writer (his book sales have surpassed 20 million copies), King has become synonymous with horror stories and movies. His many books include Carrie *(1974),* Salem's Lot *(1975),* The Shining *(1977),* The Dead Zone *(1979),* Firestarter *(1980),* Christine *(1983),* Pet Sematery *(1983),* Tommyknockers *(1984),* Misery *(1987),* Needful Things *(1991),* Insomnia *(1994),* Bag of Bones *(1998),* The Green Mile *(2000),* The Plant *(2000)—a serial novel which he published online,* The Colorado Kid *(2005), and* Cell *(2006). First published in* Playboy *in 1982, this essay explains, in the master's words, why we crave good horror shows.*

1 I think that we're all mentally ill; those of us outside the asylums only hide it a little better—and maybe not all that much better, after all. We've all known people who talk to themselves, people who sometimes squinch their faces into horrible grimaces when they believe no one is watching, people who have some hysterical fear—of snakes, the dark, the tight place, the long drop . . . and, of course, those final worms and grubs that are waiting so patiently underground.

   When we pay our four or five bucks and seat ourselves at tenth-row center in a theater showing a horror movie, we are daring the nightmare.

Why? Some of the reasons are simple and obvious. To show that we can, that we are not afraid, that we can ride this roller coaster. Which is not to say that a really good horror movie may not surprise a scream out of us at some point, the way we may scream when the roller coaster twists through a complete 360 or plows through a lake at the bottom of the drop. And horror movies, like roller coasters, have always been the special province of the young; by the time one turns 40 or 50, one's appetite for double twists or 360-degree loops may be considerably depleted.

We also go to re-establish our feelings of essential normality; the horror movie is innately conservative, even reactionary. Freda Jackson as the horrible melting woman in *Die, Monster, Die!* confirms for us that no matter how far we may be removed from the beauty of a Robert Redford or a Diana Ross, we are still light-years from true ugliness.

And we go to have fun.

Ah, but this is where the ground starts to slope away, isn't it? Because this is a very peculiar sort of fun indeed. The fun comes from seeing others menaced—sometimes killed. One critic has suggested that if pro football has become the voyeur's version of combat, then the horror film has become the modern version of the public lynching.

It is true that the mythic, "fairytale" horror film intends to take away the shades of gray. . . . It urges us to put away our more civilized and adult penchant for analysis and to become children again, seeing things in pure blacks and whites. It may be that horror movies provide psychic relief on this level because this invitation to lapse into simplicity, irrationality and even outright madness is extended so rarely. We are told we may allow our emotions a free rein . . . or no rein at all.

If we are all insane, then sanity becomes a matter of degree. If your insanity leads you to carve up women like Jack the Ripper or the Cleveland Torso Murderer, we clap you away in the funny farm (but neither of those two amateur-night surgeons was ever caught, heh-heh-heh); if, on the other hand your insanity leads you only to talk to yourself when you're under stress or to pick your nose on your morning bus, then you are left alone to go about your business . . . though it is doubtful that you will ever be invited to the best parties.

The potential lyncher is in almost all of us (excluding saints, past and present; but then, most saints have been crazy in their own ways), and every now and then, he has to be let loose to scream and roll around in the grass. Our emotions and our fears form their own body, and we recognize that it demands its own exercise to maintain proper muscle tone.

Certain of these emotional muscles are accepted—even exalted—in civilized society; they are, of course, the emotions that tend to maintain the status quo of civilization itself. Love, friendship, loyalty, kindness—these are all the emotions that we applaud, emotions that have been immortalized in the couplets of Hallmark cards and in the verses (I don't dare call it poetry) of Leonard Nimoy.

10   When we exhibit these emotions, society showers us with positive   10
reinforcement; we learn this even before we get out of diapers. When, as children, we hug our rotten little puke of a sister and give her a kiss, all the aunts and uncles smile and twit and cry, "Isn't he the sweetest little thing?" Such coveted treats as chocolate-covered graham crackers often follow. But if we deliberately slam the rotten little puke of a sister's fingers in the door, sanctions follow—angry remonstrance from parents, aunts and uncles; instead of a chocolate-covered graham cracker, a spanking.

But anticivilization emotions don't go away, and they demand periodic exercise. We have such "sick" jokes as, "What's the difference between a truckload of bowling balls and a truckload of dead babies?" (You can't unload a truckload of bowling balls with a pitchfork . . . a joke, by the way, that I heard originally from a ten-year-old.) Such a joke may surprise a laugh or a grin out of us even as we recoil, a possibility that confirms the thesis: If we share a brotherhood of man, then we also share an insanity of man. None of which is intended as a defense of either the sick joke or insanity but merely as an explanation of why the best horror films, like the best fairy tales, manage to be reactionary, anarchistic, and revolutionary all at the same time.

The mythic horror movie, like the sick joke, has a dirty job to do. It deliberately appeals to all that is worst in us. It is morbidity unchained, our most base instincts let free, our nastiest fantasies realized . . . and it all happens, fittingly enough, in the dark. For those reasons, good liberals often shy away from horror films. For myself, I like to see the most aggressive of them—*Dawn of the Dead,* for instance—as lifting a trap door in the civilized forebrain and throwing a basket of raw meat to the hungry alligators swimming around in that subterranean river beneath.

Why bother? Because it keeps them from getting out, man. It keeps them down there and me up here. It was Lennon and McCartney who said that all you need is love, and I would agree with that.

As long as you keep the gators fed.

Questions on Meaning

1. What is King's succinct, five-word explanation for why we crave horror movies? What are the three reasons that he gives to elaborate this explanation?
2. What does King—who contends that everyone is mentally ill—mean by the comment, "sanity becomes a matter of degree"?
3. What are the elements of horror films that cause "good liberals" to avoid them?

Questions on Rhetorical Strategy and Style

1. What tone does King set with his opening comment? Explain why you believe that King was being serious, exaggerating, or simply toying with his readers. What was your reaction to that comment when you *completed* the essay?
2. Reread paragraphs 1–6. How does King introduce tension into his piece with the comment, "Ah, but this is where the ground starts to slope away, isn't it"? What suggestions is he placing in the minds of his readers when he begins to speak of "a very peculiar sort of fun"?
3. Show where King uses personification to discuss human emotions and fears. What does King claim that our "anticivilization emotions" demand?

Writing Assignments

1. King believes that we all need to "keep the gators fed." Do you agree? Why are or are you not attracted to horror movies? What do you believe is their attraction? What explains the incredibly popularity of King's books?
2. King uses "sick" jokes as another example of "anticivilization" emotions. Write an essay on the role of "sick" jokes or "black humor." Why do jokes invariably surface after a horrible, widely publicized event—such as a serial killing, a devastating flood, or the tragic automobile accident of a famous person? Explain why you agree that these jokes confirm our insanity—as King does—or why you feel they serve a separate purpose, such as a coping mechanism.

Censorship Wasn't All Bad

Daniel Wolf

Daniel Wolf (1948–) has been the director of Information Assurance at the National Security Agency. The Agency is responsible for, among other things, telecommunications pertaining to Homeland Security. He was the producer of The Hunger Business, *a series on emergency aid in Africa, for British Channel 4. He is also a regular contributor to* The Spectator. *In this essay Wolf argues that Western society has not abandoned censorship at all, but instead has simply revised what is considered offensive speech.*

1 We live in a culture that at one moment celebrates stupidity as wisdom, ugliness as beauty, insensitivity as honesty, offence as virtue, yet, in the next, sees dissent from respectable opinion as a cause for suspicion and the expression of uncomfortable ideas as a crime. On 31 January the government was busily trying to ram its Racial and Religious Hatred Bill through the Commons—a measure which is both unnecessary and a dangerous infringement of free speech. It suffered a well-merited defeat. Meanwhile, all around us, those same hard-won, fragile freedoms are exploited by tabloid witch-hunts, by Celebrity Big Brother and, of course, by the vast bran-tub of masturbatory imagery and random, often incorrect, information that is the internet.

Any assault on freedom today takes place against a background of unprecedented licence. To most, there is no contradiction here. According to our prevailing philosophy of banal romanticism—designed by figures such as Rousseau, Caspar David Friedrich and Blake, and refracted through Jack Kerouac, John Lennon, Hugh Hefner, along with a multitude of others—we should all do what we feel like doing, as long as no one else gets hurt in the process. Of course, quite a lot of people do get hurt but no one is keeping the score. It is an axiom of our age that desire trumps all considerations and, in virtually any newspaper or magazine you open, you can stumble over sentences like, 'it just felt so right' or, 'I had to follow my heart'.

As we anxiously observe the world through the spectacles of a sex-crazed adolescent, our commitment to liberty is vitiated by our terror of truth: in theory we can say what we like but, if we do, we are pilloried by an army of busybodies, seeking to ensure that we do not think the wrong thoughts, say the wrong things, use the wrong language. The general taboo against explicit sexual material, which operated before the 1960s, has been replaced by a more restrictive form of censorship, a haunting fear of causing offence. We may have pornography on demand, but we are more frightened of our own thoughts, and others' words, than an army of Victorian matrons.

Perhaps that's what happens when freedom becomes licence. Edmund Burke was on to the problem: 'Men are qualified for civil liberty in exact proportion to their disposition to put moral chains upon their own appetites; in proportion as their love to justice is above their rapacity; in proportion as their soundness and sobriety of understanding is above their vanity and presumption. . . . Society cannot exist unless a controlling power upon will and appetite be placed somewhere, and the less of it there is within, the more there must be without. It is ordained in the eternal constitution of things that men of intemperate minds cannot be free. Their passions forge their fetters.'

5   Over the past half-century, the Western world—and increasingly   5
the whole world—has been subjected to an unprecedented experiment in mind manipulation. The internet is only the latest turn of the screw. Modern media bombard us from every angle with powerful images and sounds, emotive pictures, dramatic and frequently unfounded claims. The common defence of this Niagara of inane, sometimes vicious, chatter presents it as both the cost and the benefit of free speech, offered to us for our entertainment in a spirit of democratic egalitarianism. However, we, the audience for this speech, are also shaped by it, in an endless reverberation which works to rob us of our sense of discrimination and judgment, not to mention our time and energies.

It's the vice of the present to believe that everything is better the way it is. It ain't necessarily so. Before the rise of modem media, there was censorship, formal and informal, but it did not cripple the intellectual life of the country, as libertarians on both the Left and Right maintain. In the world before the 1960s, what mattered could be easily said, and what couldn't be said rarely deserved the effort expended to bring it into the light. You may not have wanted to give Lady Chatterley's Lover to your wife or servant (in the memorable words of Mervyn Griffith-Jones, QC), but only because the book was so dull.

The formal machinery of censorship amounted in practice to occasional interventions by the Lord Chamberlain's office, the odd D-Notice and the rarely invoked Obscene Publications Act. If you wanted to read Lady Chatterley's Lover or Ulysses before the bans were lifted, you did so without risk or great difficulty. The cinema was more thoroughly controlled, but this was due to the industry's own nervous embrace of self-regulation. The increase in the explicitness of films over the last 40 years has had equivocal benefits: we have gained in verisimilitude but we have lost the power of implication.

Censorship in Britain was not, as some would have it, the 'ultimate obscenity'. It was a clumsy, ramshackle way of expressing the sense, shared by almost the whole of society, that some experiences were best left to the imagination. It is mere arrogance to insist that because we have learnt to make public what was once thought private, to make explicit what was once implied, to overcome inhibition and abolish illusion, we are, in any useful sense, wiser, stronger, more truthful than our parents and grandparents.

More fundamentally, to think that we have reached new heights of freedom, and therefore perfection, because we have lost a measure of restraint is a classic error. Free speech today, in the absence of censorship, is as thoroughly policed as it ever was in the days before the rise of television and the internet, perhaps more so. As the government exploits public indifference towards the essential principles of a free society, controversial views are classified as 'unacceptable' and 'inappropriate' by a host of interest groups. Meanwhile the collection of personal information in our wired world promises an age of social control quite unlike anything we have seen before. De Tocqueville's 'tyranny of the majority' (and sometimes of the minority) may triumph more completely, more pervasively than he ever imagined.

10   The news that Google, the search engine, is collaborating with the   10
Chinese authorities in censoring internet access in their country could
stand as a symbol of the superficiality of our belief in open debate.
That belief can easily be set aside, it seems, if what is said may offend
some important group, whether it is a dictatorial government abroad
or a noisy and threatening lobby at home. If we want to take credit for
our belief in free speech, it needs to be genuinely free; if we have to
bear the cost of Celebrity Big Brother, let's at least reap the benefit of
saying what's on our minds, rather than slumping in silence, suffo-
cated by our lethargy, timidity and poisonous cynicism.

Questions on Meaning

1. How does Wolf characterize the current assault on free speech? How is it different from restrictions before the 1960s?
2. What is the "unprecedented experiment in mind manipulation" to which Wolf refers in paragraph five? To what extent do you agree or disagree with this idea?
3. How has technology affected freedom of speech, according to Wolf?

Questions on Rhetorical Strategy and Style

1. One element of effective persuasion is an appeal to authority. How does the extensive quotation from political philosopher Edmund Burke support Wolf's argument?
2. Wolf begins with a series of contrasts: stupidity vs. wisdom, ugliness vs. beauty, insensitivity vs. honesty, offense vs. virtue. How do these contrasts establish a pattern for the rest of the article? Identify other key instances of contrast in the article and explain their significance to its impact.
3. Two of the key terms in Wolf's argument are *freedom* and *licence* (*license* in American spelling). Find definitions of these terms in a comprehensive dictionary and explain how their essential differences are reflected in Wolf's article.

Writing Assignments

1. Wolf's reply to the idea things are better today is, "It ain't necessarily so." Consider how things have changed in your lifetime (in technology, music, education, government regulations) and write an essay either supporting or refuting his position.
2. Wolf does not use the term, but implicit in his article is a critique of "political correctness." Write an essay explaining your own understanding of the term. To what extent do you feel that it aptly describes the current social climate? To what extent do you feel that the term is used to silence those who espouse unpopular positions?
3. Wolf refers to two famous cases of literary censorship in England: D. H. Lawrence's *Lady Chatterley's Lover* and James Joyce's *Ulysses*. Research these two cases in the United States and write a report highlighting the key issues involved. How did these cases reflect prevailing attitudes about sexual content in literature?

The Beast in the Jungle
Henry James

Henry James (1843-1916) was born into a wealthy family. He was privately educated until 1855 and spent the next five years in Europe traveling with his family and continuing his education, returning to Newport, Rhode Island in 1860. He attended Harvard Law School but dropped out to work as an essayist, reviewer, and novelist. His novels—including Washington Square *(1880),* Portrait of a Lady *(1881),* Turn of the Screw *(1898), and* The Wings of the Dove *(1902)—are complex and subtle portraits of manners and mores, often depicting contrasts between Europeans and Americans. In this story, James describes a type of character who often appears in his work: an oversensitive young man who is afraid of life.*

I

1   What determined the speech that startled him in the course of their encounter scarcely matters, being probably but some words spoken by himself quite without intention— spoken as they lingered and slowly moved together after their renewal of acquaintance. He had been conveyed by friends an hour or two before to the house at which she was staying; the party of visitors at the other house, of whom he was one, and thanks to whom it was his theory, as always, that he was lost in the crowd, had been invited over to luncheon. There had been after luncheon much dispersal, all in the interest of the original motive, a view of Weatherend itself and the fine things, intrinsic features, pictures, heirlooms, treasures of all the arts,

that made the place almost famous; and the great rooms were so numerous that guests could wander at their will, hang back from the principal group and in cases where they took such matters with the last seriousness give themselves up to mysterious appreciations and measurements. There were persons to be observed, singly or in couples, bending toward objects in out-of-the-way corners with their hands on their knees and their heads nodding quite as with the emphasis of an excited sense of smell. When they were two they either mingled their sounds of ecstasy or melted into silences of even deeper import, so that there were aspects of the occasion that gave it for Marcher much the air of the "look around," previous to a sale highly advertised, that excites or quenches, as may be, the dream of acquisition. The dream of acquisition at Weatherend would have had to be wild indeed, and John Marcher found himself, among such suggestions, disconcerted almost equally by the presence of those who knew too much and by that of those who knew nothing. The great rooms caused so much poetry and history to press upon him that he needed some straying apart to feel in a proper relation with them, though this impulse was not, as happened, like the gloating of some of his companions, to be compared to the movements of a dog sniffing a cupboard. It had an issue promptly enough in a direction that was not to have been calculated.

It led, briefly, in the course of the October afternoon, to his closer meeting with May Bartram, whose face, a reminder, yet not quite a remembrance, as they sat much separated at a very long table, had begun merely by troubling him rather pleasantly. It affected him as the sequel of something of which he had lost the beginning. He knew it, and for the time quite welcomed it, as a continuation, but didn't know what it continued, which was an interest or an amusement the greater as he was also somehow aware—yet without a direct sign from her—that the young woman herself hadn't lost the thread. She hadn't lost it, but she wouldn't give it back to him, he saw, without some putting forth of his hand for it; and he not only saw that, but saw several things more, things odd enough in the light of the fact that at the moment some accident of grouping brought them face to face he was still merely fumbling with the idea that any contact between them in the past would have had no importance. If it had had no importance he scarcely knew why his actual impression of her should so seem to have so much; the answer to which, however, was that in such a life as they all appeared to be leading for the moment one could but take things as they came. He was satisfied, without in the least being able to say why, that this young lady might roughly have ranked in the house as a poor relation; satisfied also that she was not there on a brief visit, but was more or less a part of the establishment—almost a working, a remunerated part. Didn't she enjoy at periods a protection that she paid for by helping, among other services, to show the place and explain it, deal with the tiresome people, answer questions about the dates of the building, the styles of the furniture, the authorship of the pictures, the favourite haunts of the ghost? It wasn't that she looked as if you could have given her shillings—it was impossible to look less so. Yet when she finally drifted toward him, distinctly handsome, though ever so much older–older than when he had seen her before—it might have been as an effect of her guessing that he had, within the couple of hours, devoted more imagination to her than to all the others put together, and had thereby penetrated to a kind of truth that the others were too stupid for. She *was* there on harder terms than any one; she was there as a consequence of things suffered, one way and another, in the interval of years; and she remembered him very much as she was remembered—only a good deal better.

By the time they at last thus came to speech they were alone in one of the rooms—remarkable for a fine portrait over the chimney-place—out of which their friends had passed, and the charm of it was that even before they had spoken they had practically arranged with each other to stay behind for talk. The charm, happily, was in other things too—partly in there being scarce a spot at Weatherend without something to stay behind for. It was in the way the autumn day looked into the high windows as it waned; the way the red light, breaking at the close from under a low sombre sky, reached out in a long shaft and played over old wainscots, old tapestry, old gold, old colour. It was most of all perhaps in at the way she came to him as if, since she had been turned on to deal with the simpler sort, he might, should he choose to keep the whole thing down, just take her mild attention for a part of her general business. As soon as he heard her voice, however, the gap was filled up and the missing link supplied; the slight irony he divined in her attitude lost its advantage. He almost jumped at it to get there before her. "I met you years and years ago in Rome. I remember all about it." She confessed to disappointment—she had been so sure he didn't; and to prove how well he did he began to pour forth the particular recollections that popped up as he called for them. Her face and her voice, all at his service now, worked the miracle—the impression operating like the torch of a lamplighter who touches into flame, one by one, a long row of gas-jets. Marcher flattered himself the illumination was brilliant, yet he was really still more pleased on her showing him, with amusement, that in his haste to make everything right he had got most things rather wrong. It hadn't been at Rome—it had been at Naples; and it hadn't been eight years before—it had been more nearly ten. She hadn't been, either, with her uncle and aunt, but with her mother and her brother; in addition to which it was not with the Pembles *he* had been, but with the Boyers, coming down in their company from Rome—a point on which she insisted, a little to his confusion, and as to which she had her evidence in hand. The Boyers she had known, but didn't know the Pembles, though she had heard of them, and it was the people he was with who had made them acquainted. The incident of the thunderstorm that had raged round them with such violence as to drive them for refuge into an excavation—this incident had not occurred at the Palace of the Caesars, but at Pompeii, on an occasion when they had been present there at an important find.

He accepted her amendments, he enjoyed her corrections, though the moral of them was, she pointed out, that he *really* didn't remember the least thing about her; and he only felt it as a drawback that when all was made strictly historic there didn't appear much of anything left. They lingered together still, she neglecting her office—for from the moment he was so clever she had no proper right to him—and both neglecting the house, just waiting as to see if a memory or two more wouldn't again breathe on them. It hadn't taken them many minutes, after all, to put down on the table, like the cards of a pack, those that constituted their respective hands; only what came out was that the pack was unfortunately not perfect—that the past, invoked, invited, encouraged, could give them, naturally, no more than it had. It had made them anciently meet—her at twenty, him at twenty-five; but nothing was so strange, they seemed to say to each other, as that, while so occupied, it hadn't done a little more for them. They looked at each other as with the feeling of an occasion missed; the present would have been so much better if the other, in the far distance, in the foreign land, hadn't been so stupidly meagre. There weren't apparently, all counted, more than a dozen little old things that had succeeded in coming to pass between them; trivialities of youth, simplicities of freshness, stupidities of ignorance, small possible germs, but too deeply buried—too deeply (didn't it seem?) to sprout after so many years. Marcher could only feel he ought to have rendered her some service—saved her from a capsized boat in the Bay or at least recovered her dressing-bag, filched from her cab in the streets of Naples by a lazzarone with a stiletto. Or it would have been nice if he could have been taken with fever all alone at his hotel, and she could have come to look after him, to write to his people, to drive him out in convalescence. *Then* they would be in possession of the something or other that their actual show seemed to lack. It yet somehow presented itself, this show, as too good to be spoiled; so that they were reduced for a few minutes more to wondering a little helplessly why—since they seemed to know a certain number of the same people—their reunion had been so long averted. They didn't use that name for it, but their delay from minute to minute to join the others was a kind of confession that they didn't quite want it to be a failure. Their attempted supposition of reasons for their not having met but showed how little they knew of each other. There came in fact a moment when Marcher felt a positive pang. It was vain to pretend she was an old friend, for all the communities were wanting, in spite of which it was as an old friend that he saw she would have suited him. He had new ones enough—was surrounded with them for instance on the stage of the other house; as a new one he probably wouldn't have so much as noticed her. He would have liked to invent something, get her to make-believe with him that some passage of a romantic or critical kind *had* originally occurred. He was really almost reaching out in imagination—as against time—for something that would do, and saying to himself that if it didn't come this sketch of a fresh start would show for quite awkwardly bungled. They would separate, and now for no second or no third chance. They would have tried and not succeeded. Then it was, just at the turn, as he afterwards made it out to himself, that, everything else failing, she herself decided to take up the case and, as it were, save the situation. He felt as soon as she spoke that she had been consciously keeping back what she said and hoping to get on without it; a scruple in her that immensely touched him when, by the end of three or four minutes more, he was able to measure it. What she brought out, at any rate, quite cleared the air and supplied the link— the link it was so odd he should frivolously have managed to lose.

5 "You know you told me something I've never forgotten and that 5
again and again has made me think of you since; it was that tremendously hot day when we went to Sorrento, across the bay, for the
breeze. What I allude to was what you said to me, on the way back,
as we sat under the awning of the boat enjoying the cool. Have you
forgotten?"

He had forgotten and was even more surprised than ashamed. But
the great thing was that he saw in this no vulgar reminder of any
"sweet" speech. The vanity of women had long memories, but she was
making no claim on him of a compliment or a mistake. With another
woman, a totally different one, he might have feared the recall possibly of even some imbecile "offer." So, in having to say that he had indeed forgotten, he was conscious rather of a loss than of a gain; he
already saw an interest in the matter of her mention. "I try to think—
but I give it up. Yet I remember the Sorrento day."

"I'm not very sure you do." May Bartram after a moment said;
"and I'm not very sure I ought to want you to. It's dreadful to bring a
person back at any time to what he was ten years before. If you've lived
away from it," she smiled, "so much the better."

"Ah if *you* haven't why should I?" he asked.

"Lived away, you mean, from what I myself was?"

10 "From what *I* was. I was of course an ass," Marcher went on; "but 10
I would rather know from you just the sort of ass I was than—from
the moment you have something in your mind—not know anything."

Still, however, she hesitated. "But if you've completely ceased to
be that sort—?"

"Why I can then all the more bear to know. Besides, perhaps I
haven't."

"Perhaps. Yet if you haven't," she added. "I should suppose you'd
remember. Not indeed that *I* in the least connect with my impression
the invidious name you use. If I had only thought you foolish," she
explained, "the thing I speak of wouldn't so have remained with me.
It was about yourself." She waited as if it might come to him; but as,
only meeting her eyes in wonder, he gave no sign, she burnt her ships.
"Has it ever happened?"

Then it was that, while he continued to stare, a light broke for
him and the blood slowly came to his face, which began to burn with
recognition. "Do you mean I told you—?" But he faltered, lest what
came to him shouldn't be right, lest he should only give himself away.

15   "It was something about yourself that it was natural one should-   15
n't forget—that is if one remembered you at all. That's why I ask you,"
she smiled, "if the thing you then spoke of has ever come to pass?"

Oh then he saw, but he was lost in wonder and found himself em-
barrassed. This, he also saw, made her sorry for him, as if her allusion
had been a mistake. It took him but a moment, however, to feel it had-
n't been, much as it had been a surprise. After the first little shock of
it her knowledge on the contrary began, even if rather strangely, to
taste sweet to him. She was the only other person in the world then
who would have it, and she had had it all these years, while the fact
of his having so breathed his secret had unaccountably faded from
him. No wonder they couldn't have met as if nothing had happened.
"I judge," he finally said, "that I know what you mean. Only I had
strangely enough lost any sense of having taken you so far into my
confidence."

"Is it because you've taken so many others as well?"

"I've taken nobody. Not a creature since then."

"So that I'm the only person who knows?"

20   "The only person in the world."   20

"Well," she quickly replied, "I myself have never spoken. I've
never, never repeated of you what you told me." She looked at him so
that he perfectly believed her. Their eyes met over it in such a way that
he was without a doubt. "And I never will."

She spoke with an earnestness that, as if almost excessive, put him
at ease about her possible derision. Somehow the whole question was
a new luxury to him—that is from the moment she was in possession.
If she didn't take the sarcastic view she clearly took the sympathetic,
and that was what he had had, in all the long time, from no one
whomsoever. What he felt was that he couldn't at present have begun
to tell her, and yet could profit perhaps exquisitely by the accident of
having done so of old. "Please don't then. We're just right as it is."

"Oh I am," she laughed, "if you are!" To which she added: "Then
you do still feel in the same way?"

It was impossible he shouldn't take to himself that she was really
interested, though it all kept coming as perfect surprise. He had
thought of himself so long as abominably alone, and lo he wasn't alone
a bit. He hadn't been, it appeared, for an hour—since those moments
on the Sorrento boat. It was *she* who had been, he seemed to see as he
looked at her—she who had been made so by the graceless fact of his

lapse of fidelity. To tell her what he had told her—what had it been but to ask something of her? something that she had given, in her charity, without his having, by a remembrance, by a return of the spirit, failing another encounter, so much as thanked her. What he had asked of her had been simply at first not to laugh at him. She had beautifully not done so for ten years, and she was not doing so now. So he had endless gratitude to make up. Only for that he must see just how he had figured to her. "What, exactly, was the account I gave—?"

25   "Of the way you did feel? Well, it was very simple. You said you 25 had had from the earliest time, as the deepest thing within you, the sense of being kept for something rare and strange, possible prodigious and terrible, that was sooner or later to happen to you, that you had in your bones the foreboding and the conviction of, and that would perhaps overwhelm you."

"Do you call that very simple?" John Marcher asked.

She thought a moment. "It was perhaps because I seemed, as you spoke, to understand it."

"You do understand it?" he eagerly asked.

Again she kept her kind eyes on him. "You still have the belief?"

30   "Oh!" he exclaimed helplessly. There was too much to say. 30

"Whatever it's to be," she clearly made out, "it hasn't yet come."

He shook his head in complete surrender now. "It hasn't yet come. Only, you know, it isn't anything I'm to *do*, to achieve in the world, to be distinguished or admired for. I'm not such an ass as *that*. It would be much better, no doubt, if I were."

"It's to be something you're merely to suffer?"

"Well, say to wait for—to have to meet, to face, to see suddenly break out in my life; possibly destroying all further consciousness, possibly annihilating me; possibly, on the other hand, only altering everything, striking at the root of all my world and leaving me to the consequences, however they shape themselves."

35   She took this in, but the light in her eyes continued for him not 35 to be that of mockery. "Isn't what you describe perhaps but the expectation—or at any rate the sense of danger, familiar to so many people—of falling in love?"

John Marcher wondered. "Did you ask me that before?"

"No—I wasn't so free-and-easy then. But it's what strikes me now."

"Of course," he said after a moment, "it strikes you. Of course it strikes *me*. Of course what's in store for me may be no more than that. The only thing is," he went on, "that I think if it had been that I should by this time know."

"Do you mean because you've *been* in love?" And then as he but looked at her in silence: "You've been in love, and it hasn't meant such a cataclysm, hasn't proved the great affair?"

40 "Here I am, you see. It hasn't been overwhelming." 40

"Then it hasn't been love," said May Bartram.

"Well, I at least thought it was. I took it for that—I've taken it till now. It was agreeable, it was delightful, it was miserable," he explained. "But it wasn't strange. It wasn't what *my* affair's to be."

"You want something all to yourself—something that nobody else knows or *has* known?"

"It isn't a question of what I 'want'—God knows I don't want anything.

45 It's only a question of the apprehension that haunts me—that I 45 live with day by day."

He said this so lucidly and consistently that he could see it further impose itself. If she hadn't been interested before she'd have been interested now. "Is it a sense of coming violence?"

Evidently now too again he liked to talk of it. "I don't think of it as —when it does come—necessarily violent. I only think of it as natural and as of course above all unmistakeable. I think of it simply as *the* thing. *The* thing will of itself appear natural."

"Then how will it appear strange?"

Marcher bethought himself. "It won't—to *me*."

50 "To whom then?" 50

"Well," he replied, smiling at last, "say to you."

"Oh then I'm to be present?"

"Why you *are* present—since you know."

"I see." She turned it over. "But I mean at the catastrophe."

55 At this, for a minute, their lightness gave way to their gravity; it 55 was as if the long look they exchanged held them together. "It will only depend on yourself—if you'll watch with me."

"Are you afraid?" she asked.

"Don't leave me *now*," he went on.

"Are you afraid?" she repeated.

"Do you think me simply out of my mind?" he pursued instead of answering. "Do I merely strike you as a harmless lunatic?"

60 "No," said May Bartram. "I understand you. I believe you." 60

"You mean you feel how my obsession—poor old thing!—may correspond to some possible reality?"

"To some possible reality."

"Then you *will* watch me?"

She hesitated, then for the third time put her question. "Are you afraid?"

65 "Did I tell you I was—at Naples?" 65

"No, you said nothing about it."

"Then I don't know. And I should *like* to know," said John Marcher. "You'll tell me yourself whether you think so. If you'll watch with me you'll see."

"Very good then." They had been moving by this time across the room, and at the door, before passing out, they paused as for the full wind-up of their understanding. "I'll watch with you," said May Bartram.

II

The fact that she "knew"—knew and yet neither chaffed him nor betrayed him—had in a short time begun to constitute between them a goodly bond, which became more marked when, within the year that followed their afternoon at Weatherend, the opportunities for meeting multiplied. The event that thus promoted these occasions was the death of the ancient lady her great-aunt, under whose wing, since losing her mother, she had to such an extent found shelter, and who, though but the widowed mother of the new successor to the property, had succeeded—thanks to a high tone and a high temper—in not forfeiting the supreme position at the great house. The deposition of this personage arrived but with her death, which, followed by many changes, made in particular a difference for the young woman in whom Marcher's expert attention had recognised from the first a dependent with pride that might ache though it didn't bristle. Nothing for a long time had made him easier than the thought that the aching must have been much soothed by Miss Bartram's now finding herself able to set up a small home in London. She had acquired property, to an amount that made that luxury just possible, under her aunt's extremely complicated will, and when the whole matter began to be straightened out, which indeed took time, she let him know that the happy issue was at last in view. He had seen her again before that day, both because she had more than once accompanied the ancient lady to town and because he had paid another visit to the friends who so conveniently made of Weatherend one of the charms of their own hospitality. These friends had taken him back there; he had achieved there again with Miss Bartram some quiet detachment; and he had in London succeeded in persuading her to more than one brief absence from her aunt. They went together, on these latter occasions, to the National Gallery and the South Kensington Museum, where, among vivid reminders, they talked of Italy at large—not now attempting to recover, as at first, the taste of their youth and their ignorance. That recovery, the first day at Weatherend, had served its purpose well, had given them quite enough; so that they were, to Marcher's sense, no longer hovering about the headwaters of their stream, but had felt their boat pushed sharply off and down the current.

70 They were literally afloat together; for our gentleman this was 70 marked, quite as marked as that the fortunate cause of it was just the buried treasure of her knowledge. He had with his own hands dug up this little hoard, brought to light—that is to within reach of the dim day constituted by their discretions and privacies—the object of value the hiding-place of which he had, after putting it into the ground himself, so strangely, so long forgotten. The rare luck of his having again just stumbled on the spot made him indifferent to any other question; he would doubtless have devoted more time to the odd accident of his lapse of memory if he hadn't been moved to devote so much to the sweetness, the comfort, as he felt, for the future, that this accident itself had helped to keep fresh. It had never entered into his plan that any one should "know," and mainly for the reason that it wasn't in him to tell any one. That would have been impossible, for nothing but the amusement of a cold world would have waited on it. Since, however, a mysterious fate had opened his mouth betimes, in spite of him, he would count that a compensation and profit by it to the utmost. That the right person *should* know tempered the asperity of his secret more even than his shyness had permitted him to imagine; and May Bartram was clearly right, because—well, because there she was. Her knowledge simply settled it; he would have been sure enough by this time had she been wrong. There was that in his situa-

tion, no doubt, that disposed him too much to see her as a mere con-
fidant, taking all her light for him from the fact—the fact only—of
her interest in his predicament; from her mercy, sympathy, seriousness, her consent not to regard him as the funniest of the funny.
Aware, in fine, that her price for him was just in her giving him this
constant sense of his being admirably spared, he was careful to remember that she had also a life of her own, with things that might
happen to *her,* things that in friendship one should likewise take account of. Something fairly remarkable came to pass with him, for that
matter, in this connexion—something represented by a certain passage of his consciousness, in the suddenest way, from one extreme to
the other.

He had thought himself, so long as nobody knew, the most dis-
interested person in the world, carrying his concentrated burden, his
perpetual suspense, ever so quietly, holding his tongue about it, giving others no glimpse of it nor of its effect upon his life, asking of
them no allowance and only making on his side all those that were
asked. He hadn't disturbed people with the queerness of their having
to know a haunted man, though he had had moments of rather special temptation on hearing them say they were forsooth "unsettled." If
they were as unsettled as he was—he who had never been settled for
an hour in his life—they would know what it meant. Yet it wasn't, all
the same, for him to make them, and he listened to them civilly
enough. This was why he had such good—though possibly such
rather colourless—manners; this was why, above all, he could regard
himself, in a greedy world, as decently—as in fact perhaps even a little sublimely—unselfish. Our point is accordingly that he valued this
character quite sufficiently to measure his present danger of letting it
lapse, against which he promised himself to be much on his guard. He
was quite ready, none the less, to be selfish just a little, since surely no
more charming occasion for it had come to him. "Just a little," in a
word, was just as much as Miss Bartram, taking one day with another,
would let him. He never would be in the least coercive, and would
keep well before him the lines on which consideration for her—the
very highest—ought to proceed. He would thoroughly establish the
heads under which her affairs, her requirements, her peculiarities—he
went so far as to give them the latitude of that name—would come
into their intercourse. All this naturally was a sign of how much he
took the intercourse itself for granted. There was nothing more to be

done about *that*. It simply existed; had sprung into being with her first penetrating question to him in the autumn light there at Weatherend. The real form it should have taken on the basis that stood out large was the form of their marrying. But the devil in this was that the very basis itself put marrying out of the question. His conviction, his apprehension, his obsession, in short, wasn't a privilege he could invite a woman to share; and that consequence of it was precisely what was the matter with him. Something or other lay in wait for him, amid the twists and the turns of the months and the years, like a crouching beast in the jungle. It signified little whether the crouching beast were destined to slay him or to be slain. The definite point was the inevitable spring of the creature; and the definite lesson from that was that a man of feeling didn't cause himself to be accompanied by a lady on a tiger-hunt. Such was the image under which he had ended by figuring his life.

They had at first, none the less, in the scattered hours spent together, made no allusion to that view of it; which was a sign he was handsomely alert to give that he didn't expect, that he in fact didn't care, always to be talking about it. Such a feature in one's outlook was really like a hump on one's back. The difference it made every minute of the day existed quite independently of discussion. One discussed of course *like* a hunchback, for there was always, if nothing else, the hunchback face. That remained, and she was watching him; but people watched best, as a general thing, in silence, so that such would be predominantly the manner of their vigil. Yet he didn't want, at the same time, to be tense and solemn; tense and solemn was what he imagined he too much showed for with other people. The thing to be, with the one person who knew, was easy and natural—to make the reference rather than be seeming to avoid it, to avoid it rather than be seeming to make it, and to keep it, in any case, familiar, facetious even, rather than pedantic and portentous. Some such consideration as the latter was doubtless in his mind for instance when he wrote pleasantly to Miss Bartram that perhaps the great thing he had so long felt as in the lap of the gods was no more than this circumstance, which touched him so nearly, of her acquiring a house in London. It was the first allusion they had yet again made, needing any other hitherto so little; but when she replied, after having given him the news, that she was by no means satisfied with such a trifle as the climax to so special a suspense, she almost set him wondering if she hadn't even a larger conception of singularity for him than he had for himself. He was at all events destined to become aware little by little, as time went by, that she was all the while looking at his life, judging it, measuring it, in the light of the thing she knew, which grew to be at last, with the consecration of the years, never mentioned between them save as "the real truth" about him. That had always been his own form of reference to it, but she adopted the form so quietly that, looking back at the end of a period, he knew there was no moment at which it was traceable that she had, as he might say, got inside his idea, or exchanged the attitude of beautifully indulging for that of still more beautifully believing him.

It was always open to him to accuse her of seeing him but as the most harmless of maniacs, and this, in the long run—since it covered so much ground—was his easiest description of their friendship. He had a screw loose for her, but she liked him in site of it and was practically, against the rest of the world, his kind wise keeper, unremunerated but fairly amused and, in the absence of other near ties, not disreputably occupied. The rest of the world of course thought him queer, but she, she only, knew how, and above all why, queer; which was precisely what enabled her to dispose the concealing veil in the right folds. She took his gaiety from him—since it had to pass with them for gaiety—as she took everything else; but she certainly so far justified by her unerring touch his finer sense of the degree to which he had ended by convincing her. *She* at least never spoke of the secret of his life except as "the real truth about you," and she had in fact a wonderful way of making it seem, as such, the secret of her own life too. That was in fine how he so constantly felt her as allowing for him; he couldn't on the whole call it anything else. He allowed for himself, but she, exactly, allowed still more; partly because, better placed for a sight of the matter, she traced his unhappy perversion through reaches of its course into which he could scarce follow it. He knew how he felt, but, besides knowing that, she knew how he *looked* as well; he knew each of the things of importance he was insidiously kept from doing, but she could add up the amount they made, understand how much, with a lighter weight on his spirit, he might have done, and thereby establish how, clever as he was, he fell short. Above all she was in the secret of the difference between the forms he went through— those of his little office under Government, those of caring for his modest patrimony, for his library, for his garden in the country, for the people in London whose invitations he accepted and repaid—and the detachment that reigned beneath them and that made of all behaviour, all that could in the least be called behaviour, a long act of dissimulation. What it had come to was that he wore a mask painted with the social simper, out of the eyeholes of which there looked eyes of an expression not in the least matching the other features. This the stupid world, even after years, had never more than half-discovered. It was only May Bartram who had, and she achieved, by an art indescribable, the feat of at once—or perhaps it was only alternately—meeting the eyes from in front and mingling her own vision, as from over his shoulder, with their peep through the apertures.

So while they grew older together she did watch with him, and so she let this association give shape and colour to her own existence. Beneath *her* forms as well detachment had learned to sit, and behaviour had become for her, in the social sense, a false account of herself. There was but one account of her that would have been true all the while and that she could give straight to nobody, least of all to John Marcher. Her whole attitude was a virtual statement, but the perception of that only seemed called to take its place for him as one of the many things necessarily crowded out of his consciousness. If she had moreover, like himself, to make sacrifices to their real truth, it was to be granted that her compensation might have affected her as more prompt and more natural. They had long periods, in this London time, during which, when they were together, a stranger might have listened to them without in the least pricking up his ears; on the other hand the real truth was equally liable at any moment to rise to the surface, and the auditor would then have wondered indeed what they were talking about. They had from an early hour made up their mind that society was, luckily, unintelligent, and the margin allowed them by this had fairly become one of their commonplaces. Yet there were still moments when the situation turned almost fresh—usually under the effect of some expression drawn from herself. Her expressions doubtless repeated themselves, but her intervals were generous. "What saves us, you know, is that we answer so completely to so usual an appearance; that of the man and woman whose friendship has become such a daily habit—or almost—as to be at last indispensable." That for instance was a remark she had frequently enough had occasion to make, though she had given it at different times different developments. What we are especially concerned with is the turn it happened to take from her one afternoon when he had come to see her in honour of her birthday. This anniversary had fallen on a Sunday, at a season of thick fog and general outward gloom; but he had brought her his customary offering, having known her now long enough to have established a hundred small traditions. It was one of his proofs to himself, the present he made her on her birthday, that he hadn't sunk into real selfishness. It was mostly nothing more than a small trinket, but it was always fine of its kind, and he was regularly careful to pay for it more than he thought he could afford. "Our habit saves you at least, don't you see? because it makes you, after all, for the vulgar, indistinguishable from other men. What's the most inveterate mark of men in general? Why the capacity to spend endless time with dull women—to spend it I won't say without being bored, but without minding that they are, without being driven off at a tangent by it; which comes to the same thing. I'm your dull woman, a part of the daily bread for which you pray at church. That covers your tracks more than anything."

75   "And what covers ours?" asked Marcher, whom his dull woman   75
could mostly to this extent amuse. "I see of course what you mean by your saving me, in this way and that, so far as other people are concerned—I've seen it all along. Only what is it that saves *you?* I often thin, you know, of that."

She looked as if she sometimes thought of that too, but rather in a different way. "Where other people, you mean, are concerned?"

"Well, you're really so in with me, you know—as a sort of result of my being so in with yourself. I mean of my having such an immense regard for you, being so tremendously mindful of all you've done for me. I sometimes ask myself if it's quite fair. Fair I mean to have so involved and—since one may say it—interested you. I almost feel as if you hadn't really had time to do anything else."

"Anything else but be interested?" she asked. "Ah what else does one ever want to be? If I've been 'watching' with you, as we long ago agreed I was to do, watching's always in itself an absorption."

"Oh certainly," John Marcher said, "if you hadn't had your curiosity—! Only doesn't it sometimes come to you as time goes on that your curiosity isn't being particularly repaid?"

80   May Bartram had a pause. "Do you ask that, by any chance, be-   80
cause you feel at all that yours isn't? I mean because you have to wait so long."

Oh he understood what she meant! "For the thing to happen that never does happen? For the beast to jump out? No, I'm just where I was about it. It isn't a matter as to which I can *choose,* I can decide for a change. It isn't one as to which there *can* be a change. It's in the lap of the gods. One's in the hands of one's law—there one is. As to the form the law will take, the way it will operate, that's its own affair."

"Yes," Miss Bartram replied; "of course one's fate's coming, of course it *has* come in its own form and its own way, all the while. Only, you know, the form and the way in your case were to have been—well, something so exceptional and, as one may say, so particularly *your* own."

Something in this made him look at her with suspicion. "You say 'were to *have* been,' as if in your heart you had begun to doubt."

"Oh!" she vaguely protested.

85   "As if you believed," he went on, "that nothing will now take   85 place."

She shook her head slowly but rather inscrutably. "You're far from my thought."

He continued to look at her. "What then is the matter with you?"

"Well," she said after another wait, "the matter with me is simply that I'm more sure than ever my curiosity, as you call it, will be but too well repaid."

They were frankly grave now; he had got up from his seat, had turned once more about the little drawing-room to which, year after year, he brought his inevitable topic; in which he had, as he might have said, tasted their intimate community with every sauce, where every object was as familiar to him as the things of his own house and the very carpets were worn with his fitful walk very much as the desks in old counting-houses are worn by the elbows of generations of clerks. The generations of his nervous moods had been at work there, and the place was the written history of his whole middle life. Under the impression of what his friend had just said he knew himself, for some reason, more aware of these things; which made him, after a moment, stop again before her. "Is it possibly that you've grown afraid?"

90   "Afraid?" He thought, as she repeated the word, that his question   90 had made her, a little, change colour; so that, lest he should have touched on a truth, he explained very kindly: "You remember that that was what you asked *me* long ago—that first day at Weatherend."

"Oh yes, and you told me you didn't know—that I was to see for myself. We've said little about it since, even in so long a time."

"Precisely," Marcher interposed—"quite as if it were too delicate a matter for us to make free with. Quite as if we might find, on pressure, that I *am* afraid. For then," he said, "we shouldn't, should we? quite know what to do."

She had for the time no answer to his question. "There have been days when I thought you were. Only, of course," she added, "there have been days when we have thought almost anything."

"Everything. Oh!" Marcher softly groaned as with a gasp, half-spent, at the face, more uncovered just then than it had been for a long while, of the imagination always with them. It had always had its incalculable moments of glaring out, quite as with the very eyes of the very Beast, and, used as he was to them, they could still draw from him the tribute of a sigh that rose from the depths of his being. All they had thought, first and last, rolled over him; the past seemed to have been reduced to mere barren speculation. This in fact was what the place had just struck him as so full of—the simplification of everything but the state of suspense. That remained only by seeming to hang in the void surrounding it. Even his original fear, if fear it had been, had lost itself in the desert. "I judge, however," he continued, "that you see I'm not afraid now."

95   "What I see, as I make it out, is that you've achieved something 95 almost unprecedented in the way of getting used to danger. Living with it so long and so closely you've lost your sense of it; you know it's there, but you're indifferent, and you cease even, as of old, to have to whistle in the dark. Considering what the danger is," May Bartram wound up, "I'm bound to say I don't think your attitude could well be surpassed."

John Marcher faintly smiled. "It's heroic?"

"Certainly—call it that."

It was why he would have liked indeed to call it. "I *am* then a man of courage?"

"That's what you were to show me."

100   He still, however, wondered. "But doesn't the man of courage 100 know what he's afraid of—or *not* afraid of? I don't know *that,* you see. I don't focus it. I can't name it. I only know I'm exposed."

"Yes, but exposed—how shall I say?—so directly. So intimately. That's surely enough."

"Enough to make you feel then—as what we may call the end and the upshot of our watch—that I'm not afraid?"

"You're not afraid. But it isn't," she said, "the end of our watch. That it isn't the end of yours. You've everything still to see."

"Then why haven't *you?*" he asked. He had had, all along, to-day, the sense of her keeping something back, and he still had it. As this was his first impression of that it quite made a date. The case was the more marked as she didn't at first answer; which in turn made him go on. "You know something I don't." Then his voice, for that of a man of courage, trembled a little. "You know what's to happen." Her silence, with the face she showed, was almost a confession—it made him sure. "You know, and you're afraid to tell me. It's so bad that you're afraid I'll find out."

105 All this might be true, for she did look as if, unexpectedly to her, 105 he had crossed some mystic line that she had secretly drawn round her. Yet she might, after all, not have worried; and the real climax was that he himself, in all events, needn't. "You'll never find out."

III

It was all to have made, none the less, as I have said, a date; which came out in the fact that again and again, even after long intervals, other things that passed between them wore in relation to this hour but the character of recalls and results. Its immediate effect had been indeed rather to lighten insistence—almost to provoke a reaction; as if their topic had dropped by its own weight and as if moreover, for that matter, Marcher had been visited by one of his occasional warnings against egotism. He had kept up, he felt, and very decently on the whole, his consciousness of the importance of not being selfish, and it was true that he had never sinned in that direction without promptly enough trying to press the scales the other way. He often repaired his fault, the season permitting, by inviting his friend to accompany him to the opera; and it not infrequently thus happened that, to show he didn't wish her to have but one sort of food for her mind, he was the cause of her appearing there with him a dozen nights in the month. It even happened that, seeing her home at such times, he occasionally went in with her to finish, as he called it, the evening, and, the better to make his point, sat down to the frugal but always careful little supper that awaited his pleasure. His point was made, he thought, by him not eternally insisting with her on himself; made for instance, at such hours, when it befell that, her piano at hand and each of them familiar with it, they went over passages of the opera together. It chanced to be on one of these occasions, however, that he reminded her of her not having answered a certain question he had put to her during the talk that had taken place between them on her last birthday. "What is it that saves *you*?"—saved her, he meant, from that appearance of variation from the usual human type. If he had practically escaped remark, as she pretended, by doing, in the most important particular, what most men do—find the answer to life in patching up an alliance of a sort with a woman no better than himself—how had she escaped it, and how could the alliance, such as it was, since they must suppose it had been more or less noticed, have failed to make her rather positively talked about?

"I never said," May Bartram replied, "that it hadn't made me a good deal talked about."

"Ah well then you're not 'saved.'"

"It hasn't been a question for me. If you've had your woman I've had," she said, "my man."

110 "And you mean that makes you all right?" 110

Oh it was always as if there were so much to say! "I don't know why it shouldn't make me—humanly, which is what we're speaking of—as right as it makes you."

"I see," Marcher returned. "'Humanly,' no doubt, as showing that you're living for something. Not, that is, just for me and my secret."

May Bartram smiled. "I don't pretend it exactly shows that I'm not living for you. It's my intimacy with you that's in question."

He laughed as he saw what she meant. "Yes, but since, as you say, I'm only, so far as people make out, ordinary, you're—aren't you?—no more than ordinary either. You help me to pass for a man like another. So if I *am*, as I understand you, you're not compromised. Is that it?"

115 She had another of her waits, but she spoke clearly enough. 115 "That's it. It's all that concerns me—to help you to pass for a man like another."

He was careful to acknowledge the remark handsomely. "How kind, how beautiful, you are to me! How shall I ever repay you?"

She had her last grave pause, as if there might be a choice of ways. But she chose. "By going on as you are."

It was into this going on as he was that they relapsed, and really for so long a time that the day inevitably came for a further sounding of their depths. These depths, constantly bridged over by a structure firm enough in spite of its lightness and of its occasional oscillation in the somewhat vertiginous air, invited on occasion, in the interest of their nerves, a dropping of the plummet and a measurement of the abyss. A difference had been made moreover, once for all, by the fact that she had all the while not appeared to feel the need of rebutting his charge of an idea within her that she didn't dare to express—a charge uttered just before one of the fullest of their later discussions ended. It had come up for him then that she "knew" something and that what she knew was bad—too bad to tell him. When he had spoken of it as visibly so bad that she was afraid he might find it out, her reply had left the matter too equivocal to be let alone and yet, for Marcher's special sensibility, almost too formidable again to touch. He circled about it at a distance that alternately narrowed and widened and that still wasn't much affected by the consciousness in him that there was nothing she could "know," after all, any better than he did. She had no source of knowledge he hadn't equally—except of course that she might have finer nerves. That was what women had where they were interested; they made out things, where people were concerned, that the people often couldn't have made out for themselves. Their nerves, their sensibility, their imagination, were conductors and revealers, and the beauty of May Bartram was in particular that she had given herself so to his case. He felt in these days what, oddly enough, he had never felt before, the growth of a dread of losing her by some catastrophe—some catastrophe that yet wouldn't at all be *the* catastrophe; partly because she had almost of a sudden begun to strike him as more useful to him than ever yet, and partly by reason of an appearance of uncertainty in her health, coincident and equally new. It was characteristic of the inner detachment he had hitherto so successfully cultivated and to which our whole account of him is a reference, it was characteristic that his complications, such as they were, had never yet seemed so as at this crisis to thicken about him, even to the point of making him ask himself if he were, by any chance, of a truth, within sight or sound, within touch or reach, within the immediate jurisdiction, of the thing that waited.

When the day came, as come it had to, that his friend confessed to him her fear of a deep disorder in her blood, he felt somehow the shadow of a change and the chill of a shock. He immediately began to imagine aggravation and disasters, and above all to think of her peril as the direct menace for himself of personal privation. This indeed gave him one of those partial recoveries of equanimity that were agreeable to him—it showed him that what was still first in his mind was the loss she herself might suffer. "What if she should have to die before knowing, before seeing—?" It would have been brutal, in the early stages of her trouble, to put that question to her; but it had immediately sounded for him to his own concern, and the possibility was what most made him sorry for her. If she did "know," moreover, in the sense of her having had some—what should he think?—mystical irresistible light, this would make the matter not better, but worse, inasmuch as her original adoption of his own curiosity had quite become the basis of her life. She had been living to see what would *be* to be seen, and it would quite lacerate her to have to give up before the accomplishment of the vision. These reflexions, as I say, quickened his generosity; yet, make them as he might, he saw himself, with the lapse of the period, more and more disconcerted. It lapsed for him with a strange steady sweep, and the oddest oddity was that it gave him, independently of the threat of much inconvenience, almost the only positive surprise of his career, if career it could be called, had yet offered him. She kept the house as she had never done; he had to go to her to see he—she could meet him nowhere now, though there was scarce a corner of their loved old London in which she hadn't in the past, at one time or another, done so; and he found her always seated by her fire in the deep old-fashioned chair she was less and less able to leave. He had been struck one day, after an absence exceeding his usual measure, with her suddenly looking much older to him than he had ever thought of her being; then he recognised that the suddenness was all on his side—he had just simply and suddenly noticed. She looked older because inevitably, after so many years, she *was* old, or almost; which was of course true in still greater measure of her companion. If she was old, or almost, John Marcher assuredly was, and yet it was her showing of the lesson, not his own, that brought the truth home to him. His surprises began here; when once they had begun they multiplied; they came rather with a rush; it was as if, in the oddest way in the world, they had all been kept back, sown in thick cluster, for the late afternoon of life, the time at which for people in general the unexpected has died out.

120　　One of them was that he should have caught himself—for he *had* 120
so done—*really* wondering if the great accident would take form now
as nothing more than his being condemned to see this charming
woman, this admirable friend, pass away from him. He had never so
unreservedly qualified her as while confronted in thought with such a
possibility; in spite of which there was small doubt for him that as an
answer to his long riddle the mere effacement of even so fine a feature
of his situation would be an abject anticlimax. It would represent, as
connected with his past attitude, a drop of dignity under the shadow
of which his existence could only become the most grotesque of fail-
ures. He had been far from holding it a failure—long as he had waited
for the appearance that was to make it a success. He had waited for
quite another thing, not for such a thing as that. The breath of his
good faith came short, however, as he recognised how long he had
waited, or how long at least his companion had. That she, at all events,
might be recorded as having waited in vain—this affected him sharply,
and all the more because of his at first having done little more than
amuse himself with the idea. It grew more grave as the gravity of her
condition grew, and the state of mind it produced in him, which he
himself ended by watching as if it had been some definite disfigure-
ment of his outer person, may pass for another of his surprises. This
conjoined itself still with another, the really stupefying consciousness
of a question that he would have allowed to shape itself had he dared.
What did everything mean—what, that is, did *she* mean, she and her
vain waiting and her probable death and the soundless admonition of
it all—unless that, at this time of day, it was simply, it was over-
whelmingly too late? He had never at any stage of his queer consciousness admitted the whisper of such a correction; he had never till
within these last few months been so false to his conviction as not to
hold that what was to come to him had time, whether *he* struck himself as having it or not. That at last, at last, he certainly hadn't it, to
speak of, or had it but in the scantiest measure—such, soon enough,
as things went with him, because the inference with which his old obsession had to reckon; and this was not helped to do by the more and
more confirmed appearance that the great vagueness casting the long
shadow in which he had lived had, to attest itself, almost no margin
left. Since it was in Time that he was to have met his fate, so it was in
Time that his fate was to have acted; and as he waked up to the sense
of no longer being young, which was exactly the sense of being stale,

just as that, in turn, was the sense of being weak, he waked up to another matter beside. It all hung together; they were subject, he and the great vagueness, to an equal and indivisible law. When the possibilities themselves had accordingly turned stale, when the secret of the gods had grown faint, had perhaps even quite evaporated, that, and that only, was failure. It wouldn't have been failure to be bankrupt, that, and that only, was failure. It wouldn't have been failure to be bankrupt, dishonoured, pilloried, hanged; it was failure not to be anything. And so, in the dark valley into which his path had taken its unlooked-for twist, he wondered not a little as he groped. He didn't care what awful crash might overtake him, with what ignominy or what monstrosity he might yet be associated—since he wasn't after all too utterly old to suffer—if it would only be decently proportionate to the posture he had kept, all his life, in the threatened presence of it. He had but one desire left—that he shouldn't have been "sold."

IV

Then it was that, one afternoon, while the spring of the year was young and new she met all in her own way his frankest betrayal of these alarms. He had gone in late to see her, but evening hadn't settled and she was presented to him in that long fresh light of waning April days which affects us often with a sadness sharper than the greyest hours of autumn. The week had been warm, the spring was supposed to have begun early, and May Bartram sat, for the first time in the year, without a fire; a fact that, to Marcher's sense, gave the scene of which she formed part a smooth and ultimate look, an air of knowing, in its immaculate order and cold meaningless cheer, that it would never see a fire again. Her own aspect—he could scarce have said why—intensified this note. Almost as white as wax, with the marks and signs in her face as numerous and as fine as if they had been etched by a needle, with soft white draperies relieved by a faded green scarf on the delicate tone of which the years had further refined, she was the picture of a serene and exquisite but impenetrable sphinx, whose head, or indeed all whose person, might have been powdered with silver. She was a sphinx, yet with her white petals and green fronds she might have been a lily too—only an artificial lily, wonderfully imitated and constantly kept, without dust or stain, though not exempt from a slight droop and a complexity of faint creases, under some clear glass bell. The perfection of household care, of high polish and finish, always reigned in her rooms, but they now looked most as if everything had been wound up, tucked in, put away, so that she might sit with folded hands and with nothing more to do. She was "out of it," to Marcher's vision; her work was over; she communicated with him as across some gulf or from some island of rest that she had already reached, and it made him feel strangely abandoned. Was it— or rather wasn't it—that if for so long she had been watching with him the answer to their question must have swum into her ken and taken on its name, so that her occupation was verily gone? He had as much as charged her with this in saying to her, many months before, that she even then knew something she was keeping from him. It was a point he had never since ventured to press, vaguely fearing as he did that it might come a difference, perhaps a disagreement, between them. He had in this later time turned nervous, which was what he in all the other years had never been; and the oddity was that his nervousness should have waited till he had begun to doubt it, should have held off so long as he was sure. There was something, it seemed to him, that the wrong word would bring down on his head, something that would so at least ease off his tension. But he wanted not to speak the wrong word; that would make everything ugly. He wanted the knowledge he lacked to drop on him, if drop it could, by its own august weight. If she was to forsake him it was surely for her to take leave. This was why he didn't directly ask her again what she knew; but it was also why, approaching the matter from another side, he said to her in the course of his visit: "What do you regard as the very worst that at this time of day *can* happen to me?"

He had asked her that in the past often enough; they had, with the odd irregular rhythm of their intensities and avoidances, exchanged ideas about it and then had seen the ideas washed away by cool intervals, washed like figures traced in sea-sand. It had ever been the mark of their talk that the oldest allusions in it required but a little dismissal and reaction to come out again, sounding for the hour as new. She could thus at present meet his enquiry quite freshly and patiently. "Oh yes, I've repeatedly thought, only it always seemed to me of old that I couldn't quite make up my mind. I thought of dreadful things, between which it was difficult to choose; and so must you have done."

"Rather! I feel now as if I had scarce done anything else. I appear to myself to have spent my life in thinking of nothing *but* dreadful things. A great many of them I've at different times named to you, but there were others I couldn't name."

"They were too, too dreadful?"

"Too, too dreadful—some of them."

She looked at him a minute, and there came to him as he met it an inconsequent sense that her eyes, when one got their full clearness, were still as beautiful as they had been in youth, only beautiful with a strange cold light—a light that somehow was a part of the effect, if it wasn't rather a part of the cause, of the pale hard sweetness of the season and the hour. "And yet," she said at last, "there are horrors we've mentioned."

It deepened the strangeness to see her, as such a figure in such a picture, talk of "horrors," but she was to do in a few minutes something stranger yet—though even of this he was to take the full measure but afterwards—and the note of it already trembled. It was, for the matter of that, one of the signs that her eyes were having again the high flicker of their prime. He had to admit, however, what she said. "Oh yes, there were times when we did go far." He caught himself in the act of speaking as if it all were over. Well, he wished it were; and the consummation depended for him clearly more and more on his friend.

But she had now a soft smile, "Oh far—!"

It was oddly ironic. "Do you mean you're prepared to go further?"

She was frail and ancient and charming as she continued to look at him, yet it was rather as if she had lost the thread. "Do you consider that we went far?"

"Why I thought it the point you were just making—that we *had* looked most things in the face."

"Including each other?" She still smiled. "But you're quite right. We've had together great imaginations, often great fears; but some of them have been unspoken."

"Then the worst—we haven't faced that. I *could* face it, I believe, if I know what you think it. I feel," he explained, "as if I had lost my power to conceive such things." And he wondered if he looked as blank as he sounded. "It's spent."

"Then why do you assume," she asked, "that mine isn't?"

125   125

130   130

135   "Because you've given me signs to the contrary. It isn't a question 135
for you of conceiving, imagining, comparing. It isn't a question now
of choosing." At last he came out with it. "You know something I
don't. You've shown me that before."

These last words had affected her, he made out in a moment, ex-
ceedingly, and she spoke with firmness. "I've shown you, my dear,
nothing."

He shook his head. "You can't hide it."

"Oh, oh!" May Bartram sounded over what she couldn't hide. It
was almost a smothered groan.

"You admitted it months ago, when I spoke of it to you as of
something you were afraid I should find out. Your answer was that I
couldn't, that I wouldn't, and I don't pretend I have. But you had
something therefore in mind, and I now see how it must have been,
how it still is, the possibility that, of all possibilities, has settled itself
for you as the worst. This," he went on, "is why I appeal to you. I'm
only afraid of ignorance to-day—I'm not afraid of knowledge." And
then as for a while she said nothing: "What makes me sure is that I
see in your face and feel here, in this air and amid these appearances,
that you're out of it. You've done. You've had your experience. You
leave me to my fate."

140   Well, she listened, motionless and white in her chair, as on a de- 140
cision to be made, so that was fairly an avowal, though still, with a
small fine inner stiffness, an imperfect surrender. "It *would* be the
worst," she finally let herself say. "I mean the thing I've never said."

It hushed him a moment. "More monstrous than all the mon-
strosities we've named?"

"More monstrous. Isn't that what you sufficiently express," she
asked, "in calling it the worst?"

Marcher thought, "Assuredly—if you mean, as I do, something
that includes all the loss and all the shame that are thinkable."

"It would if it *should* happen," said May Bartram. "What we're
speaking of, remember, is only my idea."

145   "It's your belief," Marcher returned. "That's enough for me. I feel 145
your beliefs are right. Therefore if, having this one, you give me no
more light on it, you abandon me."

"No, no!" she repeated. "I'm with you—don't you see?—still."
And as to make it more vivid to him she rose from her chair—a
movement she seldom risked in these days—and showed herself, all

draped and all soft, in her fairness and slimness. "I haven't forsaken you."

It was really, in its effort against weakness, a generous assurance, and had the success of the impulse not, happily, been great, it would have touched him to pain more than pleasure. But the cold charm in her eyes had spread, as she hovered before him, to all the rest of her person, so that it was for the minute almost a recovery of youth. He couldn't pity her for that; he could only take her as she showed—as capable even yet of helping him. It was as if, at the same time, her light might at any instant go out; wherefore he must make the most of it. There passed before him with intensity the three or four things he wanted most to know; but the question that came of itself to his lips really covered the others. "Then tell me if I shall consciously suffer."

She promptly shook her head. "Never!"

It confirmed the authority he imputed to her, and it produced on him an extraordinary effect. "Well, what's better than that? Do you call that the worst?"

150 "You think nothing is better?" she asked. 150

She seemed to mean something so special that he again sharply wondered, though still with the dawn of a prospect of relief. "Why not, if one doesn't *know*?" After which, as their eyes, over his question, met in a silence, the dawn deepened and something to his purpose came prodigiously out of her very face. His own, as he took it in, suddenly flushed to the forehead, and he gasped with the force of a perception to which, on the instant, everything fitted. The sound of his gasp filled the air; then he became articulate. "I see—if I don't suffer!"

In her own look, however, was doubt, "You see what?"

"Why what you mean—what you've always meant."

She again shook her head. "What I mean isn't what I've always meant. It's different."

155 "It's something new?" 155

She hung back from it a little. "Something new. It's not what you think, see what you think."

His divination drew breath then; only her correction might be wrong. "It isn't that I *am* a blockhead?" he asked between faintness and grimness. "It isn't that it's all a mistake."

"A mistake?" she pityingly echoed. *That* possibility, for her, he saw, would be monstrous; and if she guaranteed him the immunity from pain it would accordingly not be what she had in mind. "Oh no," she declared; "it's nothing of that sort. You've been right."

Yet he couldn't help asking himself if she weren't, thus pressed, speaking but to save him. It seemed to him he should be most in a hole if his history should prove all a platitude. "Are you telling me the truth, so that I shan't have been a bigger idiot than I can bear to know? I *haven't* lived with a vain imagination, in the most besotted illusion? I haven't waited but to see the door shut in my face?"

160 She shook her head again. "However the case stands *that* isn't the 160 truth. Whatever the reality, it *is* a reality. The door isn't shut. The door's open." said May Bartram.

"Then something's to come?"

She waited once again, always with her cold sweet eyes on him. "It's never too late." She had, with her gliding step, diminished the distance between them, and she stood nearer to him, close to him, a minute, as if still charged with the unspoken. Her movement might have been for some finer emphasis of what she was at once hesitating and deciding to say. He had been standing by the chimney-piece, fireless and sparely adorned, a small perfect old French clock and two morsels of rosy Dresden constituting all its furniture; and her hand grasped the shelf while she kept him waiting, grasped it a little as for support and encouragement. She only kept him waiting, however; that is he only waited. It had become suddenly, from her movement and attitude, beautiful and vivid to him that she had something more to give him; her wasted face delicately shone with it—it glittered almost as with the white lustre of silver in her expression. She was right, incontestably, for what he saw in her face was the truth, and strangely, without consequence, while their talk of it as dreadful was still in the air, she appeared to present it as inordinately soft. This, prompting bewilderment, made him but gape the more gratefully for her revelation, so that they continued for some minutes silent, her face shining at him, her contact imponderably pressing, and his stare all kind but all expectant. The end, none the less, was that what he had expected failed to come to him. Something else took place instead, which seemed to consist at first in the mere closing of her eyes. She gave way at the same instant to a slow fine shudder, and though he remained staring—though he stared in fact but the harder—turned off and regained her chair. It was the end of what she had been intending, but it left him thinking only of that.

"Well, you don't say—?"

She had touched in her passage a bell near the chimney and had sunk back strangely pale. "I'm afraid I'm too ill."

165 "Too ill to tell me?" It sprang up sharp to him, and almost to his 165 lips, the fear she might die without giving him light. He checked himself in time from so expressing his question, but she answered as if she had heard the words.

"Don't you know—now?"

"Now—?" She had spoken as if some difference had been made within the moment. But her maid, quickly obedient to her bell, was already with them. "I know nothing." And he was afterwards to say to himself that he must have spoken with odious impatience, such an impatience as to show that, supremely disconcerted, he washed his hands of the whole question.

"Oh!" said May Bartram.

"Are you in pain?" he asked as the woman went to her.

170 "No," said May Bartram. 170

Her maid, who had put an arm round her as if to take her to her room, fixed on him eyes that appealingly contradicted her; in spite of which, however, he showed once more his mystification. "What then has happened?"

She was once more, with her companion's help, on her feet, and, feeling withdrawal imposed on him, he had blankly found his hat and gloves and had reached the door. Yet he waited for her to answer. "What *was* to," she said.

V

He came back the next day, but she was then unable to see him, and as it was literally the first time this had occurred in the long stretch of their acquaintance he turned away, defeated and sore, almost angry— or feeling at least that such a break in their custom was really the beginning of the end—and wandered alone with his thoughts, especially with the one he was least able to keep down. She was dying and he would lose her; she was dying and his life would end. He stopped in the Park, into which he had passed, and stared before him at his recurrent doubt. Away from her the doubt pressed again; in her presence he had believed her, but as he felt his forlornness he threw himself into the explanation that, nearest at hand, had most of a miserable warmth for him and least of a cold torment. She had deceived him to save him—to put him off with something in which he should be able to rest. What could the thing that was to happen to him be, after all, but just this thing that had begun to happen? Her dying, her death, his consequent solitude—*that* was what he had figured as the Beast in the Jungle, that was what had been in the lap of the gods. He had had her word for it as he left he—what else on earth could she have meant? It wasn't a thing of a monstrous order; not a fate rare and distinguished; not a stroke of fortune that overwhelmed and immortalised; it had only the stamp of the common doom. But poor Marcher at this hour judged the common doom sufficient. It would serve his turn, and even as the consummation of infinite waiting he would bend his pride to accept it. He sat down on a bench in the twilight. He hadn't been a fool. Something had *been,* as she had said, to come. Before he rose indeed it had quite struck him that the final fact really matched with the long avenue through which he had had to reach it. As sharing his suspense and as giving herself all, giving her life, to bring it to an end, she had come with him every step of the way. He had lived by her aid, and to leave her behind would be cruelly, damnably to miss her. What could be more overwhelming than that?

Well, he was to know within the week, for though she kept him a while at bay, left him restless and wretched during a series of days on each of which he asked about her only again to have a turn away, she ended his trial by receiving him where she had always received him. Yet she had been brought out at some hazard into the presence of so many of the things that were, consciously, vainly, half their past, and there was scant service left in the gentleness of her mere desire, all too visible, to check his obsession and wind up his long trouble. That was clearly what she wanted, the one thing more for her own peace while she could still put out her hand. He was so affected by her state that, once seated by her chair, he was moved to let everything go; it was she herself therefore who brought him back, took up again, before she dismissed him, her last word of the other time. She showed how she wished to leave their business in order. "I'm not sure you understood. You've nothing to wait for more. It *has* come."

Oh how he looked at her! "Really?"

"Really."

"The thing that, as you said, *was* to?"

"The thing that we began in our youth to watch for."

Face to face with her once more he believed her; it was a claim to which he had so abjectly little to oppose. "You mean that it has come as a positive definite occurrence, with a name and a date?"

180 "Positive. Definite. I don't know about the 'name,' but oh with a date!"

He found himself again too helplessly at sea. "But come in the night—come and passed me by?"

May Bartram had her strange faint smile. "Oh no, it hasn't passed you by!"

"But if I haven't been aware of it and it hasn't touched me—?"

"Ah your not being aware of it"—and she seemed to hesitate an instant to deal with this—"your not being aware of it is the strangeness *in* the strangeness. It's the wonder *of* the wonder." She spoke as with the softness almost of a sick child, yet now at last, at the end of all, with the perfect straightness of a sibyl. She visibly knew that she knew, and the effect on him was of something co-ordinate, in its high character, with the law that had ruled him. It was the true voice of the law; so on her lips would the law itself have sounded. "It *has* touched you," she went on. "It has done its office. It has made you all its own."

185 "So utterly without my knowing it?"

"So utterly without your knowing it." His hand, as he leaned to her, was on the arm of her chair, and, dimly smiling always now, she placed her own on it. "It's enough if *I* know it."

"Oh!" he confusedly breathed, as she herself of late so often had done."

"What I long ago said is true. You'll never know now, and I think you ought to be content. You've *had* it," said May Bartram.

"But had what?"

190 "Why what was to have marked you out. The proof of your law. It has acted. I'm too glad," she then bravely added, "to have been able to see what it's *not.*"

He continued to attach his eyes to her, and with the sense that it was all beyond him, and that *she* was too, he would still have sharply challenged her hadn't he so felt it an abuse of her weakness to do more than take devoutly what she gave him, take it hushed as to a revelation. If he did speak, it was out of the foreknowledge of his loneliness to come. "If you're glad of what it's 'not' it might then have been worse?"

She turned her eyes away, she looked straight before her; with which after a moment: "Well, you know our fears."

He wondered, "It's something then we never feared?"

On this slowly she turned to him. "Did we ever dream, with all our dreams, that we should sit and talk of it thus?"

195   He tried for a little to make out that they had; but it was as if their dreams, numberless enough, were in solution in some thick cold mist through which thought lost itself. "It might have been that we couldn't talk?"   195

"Well"—she did her best for him—"not from this side. This, you see," she said, "is the *other* side."

"I think," poor Marcher returned, "that all sides are the same to me." Then, however, as she gently shook her head in correction; "We mightn't, as it were, have got across—?"

"To where we are —no. We're *here*"—she made her weak emphasis.

"And much good does it do us!" was her friend's frank comment.

200   "It does us the good it can. It does us the good that *it* isn't here. 200 It's past. It's behind," said May Bartram. "Before—" but her voice dropped.

He had got up, not to tire her, but it was hard to combat his yearning. She after all told him nothing but that his light had failed—which he knew well enough without her. "Before—?" he blankly echoed.

"Before, you see, it was always to *come*. That kept it present."

"Oh I don't care what comes now! Besides," Marcher added, "it seems to me I liked it better present, as you say, than I can like it absent with *your* absence."

"Oh mine!"—and her pale hands made light of it.

205   "With the absence of everything." He had a dreadful sense of 205 standing there before her for—so far as anything but this proved, this bottomless drop was concerned—the last time of their life. It rested on him with a weight he felt he could scarce bear, and this weight it apparently was that still pressed out what remained in him of speakable protest. "I believe you; but I can't begin to pretend I understand. *Nothing,* for me, is past; nothing *will* pass till I pass myself, which I pray my stars may be soon as possible. Say, however," he added, "that I've eaten my cake, as you contend, to the last crumb—how can the thing I've never felt at all be the thing I was marked out to feel?"

She met him perhaps less directly, but she met him unperturbed. "You take your 'feelings' for granted. You were to suffer your fate. That was not necessarily to know it."

"How in the world—when what is such knowledge but suffering?"

She looked up at him a while in silence. "No—you don't understand."

"I suffer," said John Marcher.

210 "Don't, don't!" 210

"How can I help at least *that*?"

"*Don't!*" May Bartram repeated.

She spoke it in a tone so special, in spite of her weakness, that he stared an instant—stared as if some light, hitherto hidden, had shimmered across his vision. Darkness again closed over it, but the gleam had already become for him an idea. "Because I haven't the right—?"

"Don't *know*—when you needn't," she mercifully urged. "You needn't—for we shouldn't."

215 "Shouldn't ?" If he could but know what she meant! 215

"No—it's too much."

"Too much?" he still asked but, with a mystification that was the next moment of a sudden to give way. Her words, if they meant something, affected him in this light—the light also of her wasted face—as meaning *all,* and the sense of what knowledge had been for herself came over him with a rush which broke through into a question. "Is it of that then you're dying?"

She but watched him, gravely at first, as to see, with this, where he was, and she might have seen something or feared something that moved her sympathy. "I would live for you still—if I could." Her eyes closed for a little, as if, withdrawn into himself, she were for a last time trying. "But I can't!" she said as she raised them again to take leave of him.

She couldn't indeed, as but too promptly and sharply appeared, and he had no vision of her after this that was anything, but darkness and doom. They had parted for ever in that strange talk; access to her chamber of pain, rigidly guarded, was almost wholly forbidden him; he was feeling now moreover, in the face of doctors, nurses, the two or three relatives attracted doubtless by the presumption of what she had to "leave," how few were the rights, as they were called in such cases, that he had to put forward, and how odd it might even seem that their intimacy shouldn't have given him more of them. The stupidest fourth cousin had more, even though she had been nothing in such a person's life. She had been a feature of features in *his,* for what else was it to have been so indispensable? Strange beyond saying were the ways of existence, baffling for him the anomaly of his lack, as he felt it to be, of producible claim. A woman might have been, as it were, everything to him, and it might yet present him in no connexion that any one seemed held to recognise. If this was the case in these closing weeks it was the case more sharply on the occasion of the last offices rendered, in the great grey London cemetery, to what had been mortal, to what had been precious, in his friend. The concourse at her grave was not numerous, but he saw himself treated as scarce more nearly concerned with it than if there had been a thousand others. He was in short from this moment face to face with the fact that he was to profit extraordinarily little by the interest May Bartram had taken in him. He couldn't quite have said what he expected, but he hadn't surely expected this approach to a double privation. Not only had her interest failed him, but he seemed to feel himself unattended—and for a reason he couldn't seize—by the distinction, the dignity, the propriety, if nothing else, of the man markedly bereaved. It was as if in the view of society he had not *been* markedly bereaved, as if there still failed some sign or proof of it, and as if none the less his character could never be affirmed nor the deficiency ever made up. There were moments as the weeks went by when he would have liked, by some almost aggressive act, to take his stand on the intimacy of his loss, in order that it *might* be questioned and his retort, to the relief of his spirit, so recorded; but the moments of an irritation more helpless followed fast on these, the moments during which, turning things over with a good conscience but with a bare horizon, he found himself wondering if he oughtn't to have begun, so to speak, further back.

He found himself wondering at many things, and this last speculation had others to keep it company. What could he have done, after all, in her lifetime, without giving them both as it were, away? He couldn't have made known she was watching him, for that would have published the superstition of the Beast. This was what closed his mouth now—now that the Jungle had been threshed to vacancy and that the Beast had stolen away. It sounded too foolish and too flat; the difference for him in this particular, the extinction in his life of the element of suspense, was such as in fact to surprise him. He could scarce have said what the effect resembled; the abrupt cessation, the positive prohibition, of music perhaps, more than anything else, in some place all adjusted and all accustomed to sonority and to attention. If he could at any rate have conceived lifting the veil from his image at some moment of the past (what had he done, after all, if not lift it to *her?*) so to do this to-day, to talk to people at large of the Jungle cleared and confide to them that he now felt it as safe, would have been not only to see them listen as to a goodwife's tale, but really to hear himself tell one. What it presently came to in truth was that poor Marcher waded through his beaten grass, where no life stirred, where no breath sounded, where no evil eye seemed to gleam from a possible lair, very much as if vaguely looking for the Beast, and still more as if acutely missing it. He walked about in an existence that had grown strangely more spacious, and, stopping fitfully in places where the undergrowth of life struck him as closer, asked himself yearningly, wondered secretly and sorely, if it would have lurked here or there. It would have at all events *sprung;* what was at least complete was his belief in the truth of the assurance given him. The change from his old sense to his new was absolute and final; what was to happen *had* so absolutely and finally happened that he was as little able to know a fear for his future as to know a hope; so absent in short was any question of anything still to come. He was to live entirely with the other question, that of his unidentified past, that of his having to see his fortune impenetrably muffled and masked.

The torment of this vision became then his occupation; he could-n't perhaps have consented to live but for the possibility of guessing. She had told him, his friend, not to guess; she had forbidden him, so far as he might, to know, and she had even in a sort denied the power in him to learn: which were so many things, precisely, to deprive him of rest. It wasn't that he wanted, he argued for fairness, that anything past and done should repeat itself; it was only that he shouldn't, as an anticlimax, have been taken sleeping so sound as not to be able to win back by an effort of thought the lost stuff of consciousness. He de-clared to himself at moments that he would either win it back or have done with consciousness for ever; he made this idea his one motive in fine, made it so much his passion that none other, to compare with it, seemed ever to have touched him. The lost stuff of consciousness be-came thus for him as a strayed or stolen child to an unappeasable fa-ther; he hunted it up and down very much as if he were knocking at doors and enquiring of the police. This was the spirit in which, inevitably, he set himself to travel; he started on a journey that was to be as long as he could make it; it danced before him that, as the other side of the globe couldn't possibly have less to say to him, it might, by a possibility of suggestion, have more. Before he quitted London, however, he made a pilgrimage to May Bartram's grave, took his way to it through the endless avenues of the grim suburban metropolis, sought it out in the wilderness of tombs, and, though he had come but for the renewal of the act of farewell, found himself, when he had at last stood by it, beguiled into long intensities. He stood for an hour, powerless to turn away and yet powerless to penetrate the darkness of death; fixing with his eyes her inscribed name and date, beating his forehead against the fact of the secret they kept, drawing his breath, while he waited, as if some sense would in pity of him rise from the stones. He kneeled on the stones, however, in vain; they kept what they concealed; and if the face of the tomb did become a face for him it was because her two names became a pair of eyes that didn't know him. He gave them a last long look, but no palest light broke.

VI

He stayed away, after this, for a year; he visited the depths of Asia, spending himself on scenes of romantic interest, of superlative sanctity; but what was present to him everywhere was that for a man who had know what *he* had known the world was vulgar and vain. The state of mind in which he had lived for so many years shone out to him, in reflexion, as a light that coloured and refined, a light beside which the glow of the East was garish cheap and thin. The terrible truth was that he had lost—with everything else—a distinction as well; the things he saw couldn't help being common when he had become common to look at them. He was simply now one of them himself—he was in the dust, without a peg for the sense of difference; and there were hours when, before the temples of gods and the sepulchres of kings, his spirit turned for nobleness of association to the barely discriminated slab in the London suburb. That had become for him, and more intensely with time and distance, his one witness of a past glory. It was all that was left to him for proof or pride, yet the past glories of Pharaohs were nothing to him as he thought of it. Small wonder then that he came back to it on the morrow of his return. He was drawn there this time as irresistibly as the other, yet with a confidence, almost, that was doubtless the effect of the many months that had elapsed. He had lived, in spite of himself, into his change of feeling, and in wandering over the earth had wandered, as might be said, from the circumference to the centre of his desert. He had settled to his safety and accepted perforce his extinction; figuring to himself, with some colour, in the likeness of certain little old men he remembered to have seen, of whom, all meagre and wizened as they might look, it was related that they had in their time fought twenty duels or been loved by ten princesses. They indeed had been wondrous for others while he was but wondrous for himself; which, however, was exactly the cause of his haste to renew the wonder by getting back, as he might put it, into his own presence. That had quickened his steps and checked his delay. If his visit was prompt it was because he had been separated so long from the part of himself that alone he now valued.

It's accordingly not false to say that he reached his goal with a certain elation and stood there again with a certain assurance. The creature beneath the sod *knew* of his rare experience, so that, strangely now, the place had lost for him its mere blankness of expression. It met him in mildness—not, as before, in mockery; it wore for him the air of conscious greeting that we find, after absence, in things that have closely belonged to us and which seem to confess of themselves to the connexion. The plot of ground, the graven tablet, the tended flowers affected him so as belonging to him that he resembled for the hour a contented landlord reviewing a piece of property. Whatever had happened—well, had happened. He had not come back this time with the vanity of that question, his former worrying "What, *what?*' now practically so spent. Yet he would none the less never again so cut himself off from the spot; he would come back to it every month, for if he did nothing else by its aid he at least held up his head. It thus grew for him, in the oddest way, a positive resource; he carried out his idea of periodical returns, which took their place at last among the most inveterate of his habits. What it all amounted to, oddly enough, was that in his finally so simplified world this garden of death gave him the few square feet of earth on which he could still most live. It was as if, being nothing anywhere else for any one, nothing even for himself, he were just everything here, and if not for a crowd of witnesses or indeed for any witness but John Marcher, then by clear right of the register that he could scan like an open page. The open page was the tomb of his friend, and *there* were the facts of the past, there the truth of his life, there the backward reaches in which he could lose himself. He did this from time to time with such effect that he seemed to wander through the old years with his hand in the arm of a companion who was, in the most extraordinary manner, his other, his younger self; and to wander, which was more extraordinary yet, round and round a third presence—not wandering she, but stationary, still, whose eyes, turning with his revolution, never ceased to follow him, and whose seat was his point, so to speak, of orientation. Thus in short he settled to live—feeding all on the sense that he once *had* lived, and dependent on it not alone for a support but for an identity.

If sufficed him in its way for months and the year elapsed; it would doubtless even have carried him further but for an accident, superficially slight, which moved him, quite in another direction, with a force beyond any of his impressions of Egypt or of India. It was a thing of the merest chance—the turn, as he afterwards felt, of a hair, though he was indeed to live to believe that if light hadn't come to him in this particular fashion it would still have come in another. He was to live to believe this, I say, though he was not to live, I may not less definitely mention, to do much else. We allow him at any rate the benefit of the conviction, struggling up for him at the end, that, whatever might have happened or not happened, he would have come round of himself to the light. The incident of an autumn day had put the match to the train laid from of old by his misery. With the light before him he knew that even of late his ache had only been smothered. It was strangely drugged, but it throbbed; at the touch it began to bleed. And the touch, in the event, was the face of a fellow mortal. This face, one grey afternoon when the leaves were thick in the alleys, looked into Marcher's own, at the cemetery, with an expression like the cut of a blade. He felt it, that is, so deep down that he winced at the steady thrust. The person who so mutely assaulted him was a figure he had noticed, on reaching his own goal, absorbed by a grave a short distance away, a grave apparently fresh, so that the emotion of the visitor would probably match it for frankness. This face alone forbade further attention, though during the time he stayed he remained vaguely conscious of his neighbour, a middle-aged man apparently, in mourning, whose bowed back, among the clustered monuments and mortuary yews, was constantly presented. Marcher's theory that these were elements in contact with which he himself revived, had suffered, on this occasion, it may be granted, a marked, an excessive check. The autumn day was dire for him as none had recently been, and he rested with a heaviness he had not yet known on the low stone table that bore May Bartram's name. He rested without power to move, as if some spring in him, some spell vouchsafed, had suddenly been broken for ever. If he could have done that moment as he wanted he would simply have stretched himself on the slab that was ready to take him, treating it as a place prepared to receive his last sleep. What in all the wide world had he now to keep awake for? He stared before him with the question, and it was then that, as one of the cemetery walks passed near him, he caught the shock of the face.

225   His neighbour at the other grave had withdrawn, as he himself, 225 with force enough in him, would have done by now, and was advancing along the path on his way to one of the gates. This brought him close, and his pace was slow, so that—and all the more as there was a kind of hunger in his look—the two men were for a minute directly confronted. Marcher knew him at once for one of the deeply stricken—a perception so sharp that nothing else in the picture comparatively lived, neither his dress, his age, nor his presumable character and class; nothing lived but the deep ravage of the features he showed. He *showed* them—that was the point; he was moved, as he passed, by some impulse that was either a signal for sympathy or, more possibly, a challenge to an opposed sorrow. He might already have been aware of our friend, might at some previous hour have noticed in him the smooth habit of the scene, with which the state of his own senses so scantly consorted, and might thereby have been stirred as by an overt discord. What Marcher was at all events conscious of was in the first place that the image of scarred passion presented to him was conscious too—of something that profaned the air; and in the second that, roused, startled, shocked, he was yet the next moment looking after it, as it went, with envy. The most extraordinary thing that had happened to him—though he had given that name to other matters as well—took place, after his immediate vague stare, as a consequence of this impression. The stranger passed, but the raw glare of his grief remained, making our friend wonder in pity what wrong, what wound it expressed, what injury not to be healed. What had the man *had,* to make him by the loss of it so bleed and yet live?

Something—and this reached him with a pang—that *he,* John Marcher, hadn't; the proof of which was precisely John Marcher's arid end. No passion had ever touched him, for this was what passion meant; he had survived and maundered and pined, but where had been *his* deep ravage? The extraordinary thing we speak of was the sudden rush of the result of this question. The sight that had just met his eyes named to him, as in letters of quick flame, something he had utterly, insanely missed, and what he had missed made these things a train of fire, made them mark themselves in an anguish of inward throbs. He had seen *outside* of his life, not learned it within, the way a woman was mourned when she had been loved for herself; such was the force of his conviction of the meaning of the stranger's face, which still flared for him as a smoky torch. It hadn't come to him, the knowledge, on the wings of experience; it had brushed him, jostled him, upset him, with the disrespect of chance, the insolence of accident. Now that the illumination had begun, however, it blazed to the zenith, and what he presently stood there gazing at was the sounded void of his life. He gazed, he drew breath, in pain; he turned in his dismay, and turning, he had before him in sharper incision than ever the open page of his story. The name on the table smote him as the passage of his neighbour had done, and what it said to him, full in the face, was that *she* was what he had missed. This was the awful thought, the answer to all the past, the vision at the dread clearness of which he grew as cold as the stone beneath him. Everything fell together, confessed, explained, overwhelmed; leaving him most of all stupefied at the blindness he had cherished. The fate he had been marked for he had met with a vengeance—he had emptied the cup to the lees; he had been the man of his time, *the* man, to whom nothing on earth was to have happened. That was the rare stroke—that was his visitation. So he saw it, as we say, in pale horror, while the pieces fitted and fitted. So *she* had seen it while he didn't, and so she served at this hour to drive the truth home. It was the truth, vivid and monstrous, that all the while he had waited the wait was itself his portion. This the companion of his vigil had at a given moment made out, and she had then offered him the chance to baffle his doom. One's doom, however, was never baffled, and on the day she told him his own had come down she had seen him but stupidly stare at the escape she offered him.

The escape would have been to love her; then, *then* he would have lived. *She* had lived—who could say now with what passion?—since she had loved him for himself; whereas he had never thought of her (ah, how it hugely glared at him!) but in the chill of his egotism and the light of her use. Her spoken words came back to him—the chain stretched and stretched. The Beast had lurked indeed, and the Beast, as its hour, had sprung; it had sprung in that twilight of the cold April when, pale, ill, wasted, but all beautiful, and perhaps even then recoverable, she had risen from her chair to stand before him and let him imaginably guess. It had sprung as he didn't guess; it had spring as she hopelessly turned from him, and the mark, by the time he left her, had fallen where it *was* to fall. He had justified his fear and achieved his fate; he had failed, with the last exactitude, of all he was to fail of; and a moan now rose to his lips as he remembered she had prayed he mightn't know. This horror of waking—*this* was knowledge, knowledge under the breath of which the very tears in his eyes seemed to freeze. Through them, none the less, he tried to fix it and hold it; he kept it there before him so that he might feel the pain. That at least, belated and bitter, had something of the taste of life. But the bitterness suddenly sickened him, and it was as if, horribly, he saw, in the truth, in the cruelty of his image, what had been appointed and done. He saw the Jungle of his life and saw the lurking Beast; then, while he looked, perceived it, as by a stir of the air, rise, huge and hideous, for the leap that was to settle him. His dark eyes darkened—it was close; and, instinctively turning, in his hallucination, to avoid it, he flung himself, face down, on the tomb.

Questions on Meaning

1. John Marcher lives his whole life in fear of the "beast," the horrifying, unknown fate he believes awaits him. Is he insane? What constitutes "insanity?"
2. Why does May Bartram decide not to directly tell Marcher what she knows about the "beast?"

Questions on Rhetorical Strategy and Style

1. James, one of the greatest novelists who have written in English, seems consistently to break a rule of narration that all writing students learn—show, don't tell. According to the rule, storytellers are supposed to present a scene dramatically, not discuss it indirectly; however, much of this story consists of reflection that occurs in the mind of the narrator. Assuming James knew what he was doing, why do you suppose he breaks that rule?
2. Consider the description in Chapter I of the house where John Marcher and May Bartram meet and the description in Chapter VI of the man Marcher meets at the cemetery. What effect do you think James intends by putting these descriptions at these points in the story?
3. Description that is withheld can be useful to a story. What is the effect of the vagueness that surrounds Marcher's fear?

Writing Assignments

1. Consult a psychology textbook to discover basic information on the psychological concepts of narcissism, paranoia, and schizophrenia. Do any of these conditions correspond with Marcher's state of mind? In an essay, explain your psychoanalysis.
2. Write an essay that explores a fear you have faced down. Remember that the cause of the fear is not so important as the effects it had on you. Try to follow the basic narrative rule of showing, not telling, and present the situation before, at the moment of crisis, and afterward.
3. Write an essay that describes the positive and negative effects that a secret has on human relationships. Note that a secret, like a fear, can affect people to a degree that is out of proportion with the apparent importance of the secret.

The Myth of Sisyphus

Albert Camus

Albert Camus (1913–1960) was born in Mondovi, Algeria (at that time a colony of France). Camus attended the University of Algeria, where he majored in philosophy. He wrote for the Alger-Republicain, *a socialist paper, between 1937 and 1939, and edited* Soir-Republicain, *another socialist paper, from 1939–1940. He moved to France during World War II, joined the Resistance, and wrote for and edited the underground publication* Combat. *A leading proponent of existentialism, Camus is perhaps best remembered for* The Rebel: An Essay on Man in Revolt *(1954), for which he received the Nobel Prize for Literature (1957). Other books by Camus include* The Myth of Sisyphus *(1942), his first collection of philosophical essays, and the novels* The Stranger *(1942),* The Plague *(1947),* The Fall *(1956), and* Exile and the Kingdom *(1957). In this story, Camus analyzes the meaning and impact of the fate of Sisyphus—a symbol of the human condition.*

1   The gods had condemned Sisyphus to ceaselessly rolling a rock to the top of a mountain, whence the stone would fall back of its own weight. They had thought with some reason that there is no more dreadful punishment than futile and hopeless labor.   1

If one believes Homer, Sisyphus was the wisest and most prudent of mortals. According to another tradition, however, he was disposed to practice the profession of highwayman. I see no contradiction in this. Opinions differ as to the reasons why he became the futile laborer of the underworld. To begin with, he is accused of a certain levity in regard to the gods. He stole their secrets. Aegina, the daughter of

Aesopus, was carried off by Jupiter. The father was shocked by that disappearance and complained to Sisyphus. He, who knew of the abduction, offered to tell about it on condition that Aesopus would give water to the citadel of Corinth. To the celestial thunderbolts he preferred the benediction of water. He was punished for this in the underworld. Homer tells us also that Sisyphus had put Death in chains. Pluto could not endure the sight of his deserted, silent empire. He dispatched the god of war, who liberated Death from the hands of her conqueror.

It is said also that Sisyphus, being near to death, rashly wanted to test his wife's love. He ordered her to cast his unburied body into the middle of the public square. Sisyphus woke up in the underworld. And there, annoyed by an obedience so contrary to human love, he obtained from Pluto permission to return to earth in order to chastise his wife. But when he had seen again the face of this world, enjoyed water and sun, warm stones and the sea, he no longer wanted to go back to the infernal darkness. Recalls, signs of anger, warnings were of no avail. Many years more he lived facing the curve of the gulf, the sparkling sea, and the smiles of earth. A decree of the gods was necessary. Mercury came and seized the impudent man by the collar and, snatching him from his joys, led him forcibly back to the underworld, where his rock was ready for him.

You have already grasped that Sisyphus is the absurd hero. He *is*, as much through his passions as through his torture. His scorn of the gods, his hatred of death, and his passion for life won him that unspeakable penalty in which the whole being is exerted toward accomplishing nothing. This is the price that must be paid for the passions of this earth. Nothing is told us about Sisyphus in the underworld. Myths are made for the imagination to breathe life into them. As for this myth, one sees merely the whole effort of a body straining to raise the huge stone, to roll it and push it up a slope a hundred times over; one sees the face screwed up, the cheek tight against the stone, the shoulder bracing the clay-covered mass, the foot wedging it, the fresh start with arms outstretched, the wholly human security of two earth-clotted hands. At the very end of his long effort measured by skyless space and time without depth, the purpose is achieved. Then Sisyphus watches the stone rush down in a few moments toward that lower world whence he will have to push it up again toward the summit. He goes back down to the plain.

5   It is during that return, that pause, that Sisyphus interests me. A   5
face that toils so close to stones is already stone itself! I see that man
going back down with a heavy yet measured step toward the torment
of which he will never know the end. That hour like a breathing-space
which returns as surely as his suffering, that is the hour of consciousness. At each of those moments when he leaves the heights and grad-
ually sinks toward the lairs of the gods, he is superior to his fate. He
is stronger than his rock.

If this myth is tragic, that is because its hero is conscious. Where
would his torture be, indeed, if at every step the hope of succeeding
upheld him? The workman of today works every day in his life at the
same tasks, and his fate is no less absurd. But it is tragic only at the
rare moments when it becomes conscious. Sisyphus, proletarian of the
gods, powerless and rebellious, knows the whole extent of his
wretched condition: it is what he thinks of during his descent. The lu-
cidity that was to constitute his torture at the same time crowns his
victory. There is no fate that cannot be surmounted by scorn.

If the descent is thus sometimes performed in sorrow, it can also
take place in joy. This word is not too much. Again I fancy Sisyphus
returning toward his rock, and the sorrow was in the beginning. When
the images of earth cling too tightly to memory, when the call of happiness becomes too insistent, it happens that melancholy rises in man's
heart: this is the rock's victory, this is the rock itself. The boundless
grief is too heavy to bear. These are our nights of Gethsemane. But
crushing truths perish from being acknowledged. Thus, Oedipus at
the outset obeys fate without knowing it. But from the moment he
knows, his tragedy begins. Yet at the same moment, blind and desperate, he realizes that the only bond linking him to the world is the
cool hand of a girl. Then a tremendous remark rings out: "Despite so
many ordeals, my advanced age and the nobility of my soul make me
conclude that all is well." Sophocles' Oedipus, like Dostoevsky's Kir-
ilov, thus gives the recipe for the absurd victory. Ancient wisdom confirms modern heroism.

One does not discover the absurd without being tempted to write
a manual of happiness. "What! by such narrow ways—?" There is but
one world, however. Happiness and the absurd are two sons of the
same earth. They are inseparable. It would be a mistake to say that

happiness necessarily springs from the absurd discovery. It happens as well that the feeling of the absurd springs from happiness. "I conclude that all is well," says Oedipus, and that remark is sacred. It echoes in the wild and limited universe of man. It teaches that all is not, has not been, exhausted. It drives out of this world a god who had come into it with dissatisfaction and a preference for futile sufferings. It makes of fate a human matter, which must be settled among men.

All Sisyphus' silent joy is contained therein. His fate belongs to him. His rock is his thing. Likewise, the absurd man, when he contemplates his torment, silences all the idols. In the universe suddenly restored to its silence, the myriad wondering little voices of the earth rise up. Unconscious, secret calls, invitations from all the faces, they are the necessary reverse and price of victory. There is no sun without shadow, and it is essential to know the night. The absurd man says yes and his effort will henceforth be unceasing. If there is a personal fate, there is no higher destiny, or at least there is but one which he concludes is inevitable and despicable. For the rest, he knows himself to be the master of his days. At that subtle moment when man glances backward over his life, Sisyphus returning toward his rock, in that slight pivoting he contemplates that series of unrelated actions which becomes his fate, created by him, combined under his memory's eye and soon sealed by his death. Thus, convinced of the wholly human origin of all that is human, a blind man eager to see who knows that the night has no end, he is still on the go. The rock is still rolling.

10 I leave Sisyphus at the foot of the mountain! One always finds 10 one's burden again. But Sisyphus teaches the higher fidelity that negates the gods and raises rocks. He too concludes that all is well. This universe henceforth without a master seems to him neither sterile nor futile. Each atom of that stone, each mineral flake of that night-filled mountain, in itself forms a world. The struggle itself toward the heights is enough to fill a man's heart. One must imagine Sisyphus happy.

Questions on Meaning

1. What is Camus' thesis for the essay? Find a number of different ways in which he states it.
2. Why does Camus see no contradiction in Sisyphus's being both wise and prudent and a highwayman? What does that reflect of Camus' view of mankind?
3. Why does Camus call Sisyphus an "absurd hero"? What was Sisyphus's passion?

Questions on Rhetorical Strategy and Style

1. Find where Camus uses a cause and effect writing strategy to explain Sisyphus's punishment.
2. Describe Camus' analysis of Sisyphus's return to the bottom of the mountain. What does Camus conclude about Sisyphus at the end of his return trip?
3. How does Camus compare and contrast absurdity and happiness? Explain why you agree or disagree that they are "sons of the same earth."

Writing Assignments

1. Consider an endless task that you have faced—a chore, a school assignment, a summer job—in which you were able to overcome absurdity with happiness. At what point did you come face-to-face with the absurdity of your toil? How did that recognition change your perspective?
2. How does Camus relate Sisyphus's fate to the human condition? Do you "imagine Sisyphus happy"? How does this essay make you feel about your lot in life?
3. Write an essay describing one of your "nights of Gethsemane." Explain what led you into despair and the agony you felt. Describe how it resolved. Were you able to put aside the "crushing truths"? If so, how?

When I Was One-and-Twenty

A. E. Housman

*Alfred Edward Housman was born in England in 1859
and died in 1936. He attended Oxford University but
failed his final examinations, probably because of an unhappy love affair, and took a job working at the Patent Office. Determined to return to the academic world, he
contributed articles to learned journals and by 1911 had
won a position as a professor of Latin at Cambridge University. Although he remained a Latin scholar all his life,
he is best remembered for his sentimental poetry, and especially for the poems of* A Shropshire Lad, *the volume from
which this poem is taken. In "When I Was One-and-
Twenty," Housman tells a sad truth about being in love
that is as hard to remember when one is older as it is to
learn when one is younger.*

1   When I was one-and-twenty   1
        I heard a wise man say,
     "Give crowns and pounds and guineas
        But not your heart away;

5   Give pearls away and rubies   5
        But keep your fancy free."
     But I was one-and-twenty,
        No use to talk to me.

When I was one-and-twenty
10   I heard him say again,
"The heart out of the bosom
    Was never given in vain;

'Tis paid with sighs a plenty
    And sold for endless rue."
15 And I am two-and-twenty,
    And oh, 'tis true, 'tis true.

Questions on Meaning

1. Summarize the poem in prose. Do your very best to change it entirely into your own words. Find out your school's or teacher's policy on plagiarism, exchange your summaries with a classmate, and discuss whether you have avoided plagiarizing. Consult with your teacher as well.

2. Using only the summary you prepared for question 4, attempt to reconstruct the original poem. Noting which parts were easiest for you to remember, speculate about what makes writing clear and effective.

Questions on Rhetorical Strategy and Style

1. Housman's poem is on the theme of lost love, yet the narrator leaves out the whole story of losing his love, revealing only that it has happened. Comment on this strategy. Would it have been more effective to insert the details of the unhappy love affair? Why?

2. Listen to some popular music and try to match the words of "When I Was One-and-Twenty" to the music and rhythm. Once you have made a close match, see if you can remember the words without looking back at the text. Does setting them to music help? How does the music change the way you perceive organization and emphasis in the poem?

Writing Assignments

1. In the sixth line, what does the word *fancy* mean? Find other words in a college dictionary that are related to fancy (e.g., start with fanciful and fantasy) and write a short essay that describes the meaning and development of the word.

2. Does twenty-one seem young or old to be having one's first unhappy love affair? Use a study to attempt to learn what age is the norm. Use a questionnaire that asks people for both simple facts (e.g., "What age were you when you first fell in love?") and open-ended narratives (e.g., "How and why did you lose your first love?") and prepare a report from your results. You'll probably get better results with your questionnaire if you allow your respondents to remain anonymous. In any case, you must tell anyone who fills out your questionnaire exactly how you plan to use the information, and you must get each person's written permission to use the responses in your research.

Sonnet 18: Shall I Compare Thee to a Summer's Day?

William Shakespeare

According to tradition, William Shakespeare was born on April 23, 1564 in Stratford-upon-Avon, England. He was the third of eight children born to John and Mary Shakespeare. At age 18, he married 26-year-old Anne Hathaway, six months before the birth of their son. Two years later, there were twins to support as well. It is well known that by the time he was 25, he was a working actor and playwright in London. When he died on his birthday in 1616, he had completed a body of work that ensured his place as the greatest poet and playwright ever to write in English. In addition to writing the nearly forty plays for the stage in London that are best known to the public, Shakespeare wrote a number of poems, including a series (or "cycle") of sonnets that includes the sonnet reprinted here. In it, Shakespeare opens with a rhetorical question, "Shall I compare thee to a summer's day," that represents a conventional kind of flattering overstatement used in love poems of the time.

1   Shall I compare thee to a summer's day?   1
Thou art more lovely and more temperate:
Rough winds do shake the darling buds of May,
And summer's lease hath all too short a date;
5   Sometime too hot the eye of heaven shines,   5
And often is his gold complexion dimmed,
And every fair from fair sometime declines,
By chance or nature's changing course untrimmed:
But thy eternal summer shall not fade,

Shall I Compare Thee To A Summer's Day? (1609)

129

10   Nor lose possession of that fair thou ow'st,   10
         Nor shall Death brag thou wand'rest in his shade,
         When in eternal lines to time thou grow'st.
            So long as men can breathe or eyes can see,
            So long lives this, and this gives life to thee.

Questions on Meaning

1. The word *untrimmed* meant "stripped of its beauty" in the Early Modern English of Shakespeare's time. Are the words *temperate*, *lease*, and *date* used in their modern senses? Look them up in a college dictionary or the *Oxford English Dictionary* and identify the definition you think is being used.
2. Paraphrase the poem, writing it as if it were a love letter. Then summarize the argument that the poet is making to his beloved. Is it logical? Persuasive? What do you think he hoped to accomplish?
3. Poets phrase their lines very economically to create rhyme and meter without sounding awkward. This sometimes results in ambiguity, as in the line "And every fair from fair sometime declines . . . ." What are the meanings of the word *fair* in that line?

Questions on Rhetorical Strategy and Style

1. Notice that the poet's argument comes in two parts—the first eight lines (called an "octave") express a sentiment and the last six lines (the "sestet") present an observation based on the sentiment. Describe the change in tone from the octave to the sestet.
2. This poem is a sonnet. That is, it consists of fourteen lines in a meter called iambic pentameter (ten syllables per line with weak and strong stress alternating from one syllable to the next). Which lines sound "poetic" to you, and which might be written as prose? Explain.

Writing Assignments

1. This sonnet is the eighteenth in a series (or "cycle") that Shakespeare wrote. Its theme is the impermanence of youth and beauty. Find the rest of the series in the library (or on the Internet at the Gutenberg electronic text site at http://www.gutenberg.net/). Read some of the sonnets and report on other themes that you find there.
2. In a book on literary terms, find the term *Petrarchan Sonnet*. Compare and contrast Shakespeare's sonnet with the Petrarchan form.